Reinventing Budgeting: The Impact of Third Way Modernisation on Local Government Budgeting

Reinventing Budgeting: The Impact of Third Way Modernisation on Local Government Budgeting

W. B. Seal and Amanda Ball*

* With research assistance from Marleen Vanstockem

ELSEVIER

AMSTERDAM • BOSTON • HEIDELBERG • LONDON
NEW YORK • OXFORD • PARIS • SAN DIEGO
SAN FRANCISCO • SINGAPORE • SYDNEY • TOKYO

CIMA Publishing is an imprint of Elsevier

CIMA PUBLISHING

CIMA Publishing is an imprint of Elsevier
Linacre House, Jordan Hill, Oxford OX2 8DP, UK
30 Corporate Drive, Suite 400, Burlington, MA 01803, USA

First edition 2008

British Library Cataloguing in Publication Data
A catalogue record for this book is available from the British Library

Library of Congress Cataloging-in-Publication Data
A catalog record for this book is available from the Library of Congress

ISBN: 978-0-7506-8981-6

For information on all CIMA publishing publications
visit our web site at books.elsevier.com

Typeset by Charon Tec Ltd., A Macmillan Company. (www.macmillansolutions.com)

Printed and bound in Great Britain

08 09 10 10 9 8 7 6 5 4 3 2 1

Contents

Researcher's Contact Details

W. B. Seal
Professor of Management Accounting
Business School
Loughborough University
Leicester
LE11 3TU
UK
E. w.b.seal@boro.ac.uk

Amanda Ball
Professor of Accounting
College of Business and Economics
University of Canterbury
Private Bag 4800
Christchurch 8020
New Zealand
E. amanda.ball@canterbury.ac.nz

Acknowledgements

The researchers are grateful for the financial support of the research board of the Chartered Institute of Management Accountants (Project No. 264) and for the help of numerous officials and members in the case local study authorities.

Executive Summary

The focus of this project was on New Labour 1997–2003 policy innovations for the sector and their impact on traditional, incrementalist budgeting practices. The most recent initiative is the 'Comprehensive Performance Assessment' (CPA) whereby the Audit Commission ranks the corporate performance of authorities rather than just evaluating individual service areas as under the 'Best Value' regime. The central question motivating the report was: *What is the extent to which it is possible or useful to reform traditional, incrementalist budgeting practices?*

The project was based on a longitudinal field study of budgetary practice in two large but very contrasting English local authorities. Officials in the Office of the Deputy Prime Minister and at the Audit Commission were also interviewed.

The main findings

- Both the case study authorities abolished departmental structures and adopted small 'cabinets' with senior members holding portfolios that reflect a cross-cutting perspective. Budget scrutiny by elected councillors was greatly streamlined.
- Both the authorities had developed long and medium term plans that were intended to indicate the councils' priorities and guide long-term financial strategies. Increased use of 'policy-led budgeting' was emerging in both the authorities.
- Both the authorities had developed new reporting systems that not only picked up the traditional budgetary variances but also monitored non-financial performance.
- Services (and their budgets) were subject to periodic fundamental reviews either as a result of Best Value or as part of a base budget review processes developed by the authorities themselves.
- Social services were pioneering cross-cutting initiatives with education and health that were beginning to influence traditional budgetary practices.
- Modernisation seemed to be associated with outsourcing rather than on a rational appraisal of "make or buy" which might suggest bringing some services back in-house.

- A schools funding crisis indicated a lack of understanding of local educational cost drivers by central government coupled with a dysfunctional approach to participatory budgeting.
- In a period when council taxes generally rose quickly, central government should have been less quick to "scapegoat" local government for problems that it had caused. On its part, local government should have tried to improve its public image in the many areas where it had re-invented itself.

List of Abbreviations

BBR	Base Budget Review
BV	Best Value
BVPP	Best Value Performance Plan
CCT	Compulsory Competitive Tendering
CIMA	The Chartered Institute of Management Accountants
CIPFA	The Chartered Institute of Public Finance and Accountancy
CPA	Comprehensive Performance Assessment
DETR	Department of the Environment, Transport and Regions
DFES	Department for Education and Skills
DTLR	Department of Local Government, Transport and Regions
EFQM	European Foundation for Quality Management
ERP	Enterprise Resource Planning
ICS	Internal Charging System
ISB	Invest to Save Budget
LEA	Local Education Authority
NPM	New Public Management
PI	Performance Indicators
PFI	Private Finance Initiative
PPA	Perfect Public Administration
PPBS	Planning, Programming, Budgeting Systems
PPP	Public–Private Partnership
PSA	Public Sector Agreement
SEN	Special Educational Needs
SSA	Standard Spending Assessment
VFM	Value for Money
ZBB	Zero Base Budget

1

Introduction: Aims, Methods and Methodologies

Local government and this research

With local expenditure 25 per cent of total public expenditure and 10 per cent of national income (Hale and Capaldi, 2003), UK local government is an economically important sector. Having responsibilities in areas such as education, social services, and environmental well-being, local government is also a major player in the delivery of public services. As a senior civil servant interviewed for this project put it:

> If you look at the [last Labour Party election] manifesto half the things have to be done by local government.

Yet local government is not just about service delivery as local authorities are democratically elected bodies and, as such, have an explicitly political dimension. This political dimension became progressively more evident as the research proceeded. At the beginning of the period, central government's main concern was to ensure that ministers were able to deliver *national* targets on public services, especially education, which was still nominally a sphere of *local* political responsibility. At the end of the period, more general issues of local government funding and taxation had culminated in demonstrations and marches (Hetherington, 2004). As Mrs. Thatcher found out with the poll tax and as New Labour discovered, the apparently unglamorous and complex topic of local government financial management has a surprising capacity for unsettling even the strongest of national governments.

The Conservative approach to reform in the period 1979–1997 tended to down play the political role of local government with an emphasis on changing the mode of service delivery through policies such as compulsory competitive tendering (CCT) and centrally imposed 'caps' on local expenditure. This constraining approach to local government was expected to change with the election of a New Labour government in 1997. With a strong tradition of local government activism and influenced by the concepts of the *Third Way* (Giddens, 1998), the new government seemed to have a much greater commitment to reforming local government rather than constraining it. Yet reform did not mean that local government was given complete license from central government scrutiny and control, as is explored in this report. Although New Labour abolished the much disliked CCT and the capping of local government expenditure, it retained reserve powers to control local expenditure and required local authorities to deliver services based on the new principles of 'Best Value'.

The importance of budgeting

Budgeting has been described as being 'at the core of the financial process within a local authority' (Hale and Capaldi, 2003, p. 309). Yet the budgeting process embraces far more than just financial management. As in a private sector organisation, budgeting involves *planning* and *control* of organisational activities. Additionally, in a democratic context, the budget also plays a key role in the political process, enabling elected members to discuss priorities on expenditure and to set local taxes and charges.

Some changes implemented by New Labour were explicitly aimed at reforming local financial management. For example the Green paper, *Modernising Local Government Finance* (DTLR, 2000) reviewed the systems of central government grants, the capital investment and borrowing requirements, taxes and charges, and consideration of changes to the business rate (Hale and Capaldi, 2003). Although there was very little explicit mention of budgeting in many of the Green and White papers on local government reform in the period studied, it was clear that policy makers were very aware of the organisational, managerial and political traditions in local authority budgeting. Modernisation policies aiming to achieve 'integration', 'cross-cutting' and 'joined-up government' (DETR, 1998) had implications for the organisational context of the budgetary cycle. Although not explicitly aimed at financial management, more general modernisation measures (DETR, 1998) began to have an impact on local authority budgeting practices through changes in the organisational and institutional context. For example, the increased use and perceived legitimacy of performance indicators and of inspection and audit systems, changes in political management structures, outsourcing and new consultation procedures all meant that the old traditions of incremental budgeting were under challenge. At the beginning of the research project, early signs of innovation included:

1. an increased use of policy-led budgeting;
2. pooled budgets between different service areas involved in common programmes;

3. outsourcing of specific services such as education with the explicit provision of open book accounting;
4. three-year financial strategies with special mechanisms to allow investment in services and promote changes in service provision.

The aim of the project

The overall aim of the project was to undertake an empirical examination of budgetary practice in two large local authorities in England. These authorities were located in quite different regions of the country and faced different economic, social and political pressures. One authority in the north of England had a declining traditional manufacturing base, high levels of unemployment and a relatively large proportion of population originating from the Indian sub-continent. The other authority was located in the south of England near to London and faced different challenges based around issues of congestion and labour shortages in the public services.

The project had five main objectives:

1. To ascertain the forms of budgeting employed by the authorities prior to the reforms introduced by the New Labour government following the 1997 election.
2. To trace the effects of changes in political and management systems such as Best Value performance frameworks and cabinet structures on the practice of budgeting.
3. To assess the impact of public/private partnerships on the practice of budgeting.
4. To examine the impact of cross-service programmes on budgeting practice.
5. To compare the two authorities and examine the emergence of innovations in council budgeting.

Reforming local budgeting

The new public management

Many recent proposals for local government modernisation in the UK seem to be informed by a widely held view that past efforts at reform have failed (Stoker, 1996). Budgeting, in particular, has been dominated by the practice of *incrementalism*. When global budget cuts or increases are required there has been a tendency to decide on across-the-board percentage decreases/increases with little attempt to develop a system of priorities. To Wildavsky (1975), incrementalism was not an easily remedied blemish but rather an understandable response in the face of the immense calculative complexity of alternative, purportedly more rational, approaches such as planning, programming, budgeting systems (PPBS) which never took root in UK government at either central or local levels.

Under a Conservative government (1979–1997), the various policies described through the umbrella term of the 'New Public Management' (NPM) (Hood, 1995; Olson *et al.*, 1998) did result in some changes in service delivery through innovations such as compulsory contractualisation but they did not change long established budgetary practices at corporate level (Walsh, 1995; Seal, 1999). In contrast, the NPM did change budgeting practice quite directly in the case of Education services (Mayston, 1998). Schools were given more power to control their own budgets but were also subject to a national curriculum and more transparent performance indicators. As subsequent chapters will show, the long term impact of the 1988 Education Act was still being worked through during the fieldwork period as modernising policies tended to reinforce the principles of *school-based* financial management freedom combined with *nationally determined* educational targets (Ezzamel *et al.*, 2007).

New labour modernisation (1997–2003)

This project has focused on tracking the impact of New Labour local government policies between 1997 and 2003. One advantage that local authorities had under New Labour was a steady increase in financial resources. On average over the six-year period, they received about 25 per cent more in real terms from the government. They were also allowed to raise more local revenue. These increases coupled with the relative stability of political and macroeconomic factors (e.g. low inflation, low unemployment) seemed to us to be a relatively favourable environment within which to introduce reforms that might weaken the propensity to budget incrementally.

Tacit acknowledgement of the resistance to modernisation was evident in government publications in which an implicitly incrementalist picture of public sector governance is revealed. For example, setting out its wider thinking on the public sector (DETR, 1999), the government presented an interesting and relatively sophisticated discussion of why parts of government may lack the desired objectives of efficiency, dynamism and effectiveness. Paradoxically, this White Paper discussion identified just those characteristics that have always defeated programmes such as Best Value. It mentions that 'public services can be organised too much around the structure of providers rather than users' (DETR, 1999, p. 11). Additionally, services may be slow to respond to detailed demands because accountability mechanisms lack fine-tuning. As the White Paper stated: 'although the public can express its dissatisfaction through the ballot box, this can be a blunt instrument, removing whole local or central governments intermittently and often not addressing underlying reasons why things are wrong' (DETR, 1999, p. 11). The budgeting system in the public sector is input oriented rather than output oriented. As a result, 'Ministers, departments and units have often been forced to devote much of their effort to maximising their funding rather than considering what difference they can make in the form of actual results or outcomes' (DETR, 1999, p. 11).

Whilst New Labour initiatives in the period 1997–2003 may not have directly addressed budgeting issues, they indirectly provided an implicit attack on traditional departmentalist attitudes. This agenda provided a useful setting in which to research the central question for this study is: *How far it is possible to reform or improve budgeting against a background of established tradition and practice?*

Research methods and methodologies

The primary research methodology was field work in two major English local authorities. The contextual contrast between the two authorities was stark. *Southshire* (an assumed name) was a county council located in a very affluent part of the country with a mixture of rural, urban and suburban areas. It had been Conservative controlled for most of the modern era. *Eastmet* (an assumed name) was a metropolitan council located in the north with high unemployment and a large population originating in the Indian subcontinent. It was generally Labour controlled but had recent periods of Conservative control. During the main part of our fieldwork, it had a hung council.

Apart from the routine observations of physical phenomena made during frequent visits to the case authorities, the research drew on two main sources of data. First, there was a wealth of documents produced by both local and central government, which, as public sector bodies, they published on the web. Although this source of data was beguiling, its very ease of access lent a potentially misleading air of rationality, intentionality and of the fulfilment of grand designs. Furthermore, websites are supremely suitable for historical revisionism leaving very little trace of previous structures and plans.

The second source of data came from interviews with central and local officials, locally elected representatives (members) and observations of budgetary committees. Anonymised semi-structured interviews and access to working committees gave insights into the less planned, less consensual and less reverential views of real organisational actors. Yet there was a link between these two types of data in that actors were either responding to the official, 'White Paper' view of their duties and/or were invited to comment on the official agenda through questioning.

In most cases, interviews were carried out by the two researchers lasting about one hour per session. This method ensured that as accurate a record as possible was kept of the interview, and helped maintain a balance in the questioning. The aim of the case study approach was to give both an *in depth* view of the impact of any budget changes and take a *longitudinal* perspective. In the light of the historical record of superficiality or unsustainable budget reforms, the fieldwork was informed by a desire to distinguish between intentions and consequences. The fieldwork period extended beyond the annual budgetary cycle and involved at least two sets of interviews with the main players after appropriate time lapses. The main interviews were with:

- Local authority senior officers and members in the two local authorities.
- Managers responsible for services at the operational level, particularly personal social and education services.
- Politicians and officials had in central government departments who had an interest in local authority budgeting.
- An official in the Audit Commission with responsibility for developing the Comprehensive Performance Assessment framework.

Comparisons and longitudinal issues

Wherever possible the approach was to replicate interviews in both authorities in order to develop comparisons. It was possible to compare budgeting practices at the corporate level and in the major service areas of education and personal social services. However, although it was possible to obtain outline permission for interviews before the project began, the levels of access in the two authorities were not identical. For example, in Eastmet, excellent details on the schools budgeting process were obtained, but access to actual service managers in social services was not. In Southshire, it was not possible to get the same access to schools budgeting, but there was better contact with non-financial service managers.

In terms of longitudinal issues, two problems that emerged led to a slight extension to the project time span. First, schools ran into severe budgetary difficulties, especially in Southshire. Second, changes in the distribution of central government grant and unanticipated rises in costs saw politically explosive rises in council tax. Although it was recognised that there was a need to impose a time constraint on the research, the time extension presented an opportunity to assess local and central government responses to these budgetary problems.

Although the two cases were not intended to generate statistically significant results, the report analyses some numerical data from the case authorities which means it has been possible to triangulate the interview and documentary evidence (Scapens, 1990).

Conclusions

In conclusion, this chapter has set out the research approach and background to the study, and the main themes of the report have been introduced. Budgeting has been identified as a core process in local government political and financial management. For understandable reasons to do with the complexity of identifying budget priorities, public sector budgeting has been dominated by incrementalism: the practice of global, across-the-board percentage decreases/increases in the organisation's budget. The central question motivating the report was: *What is the extent to which it is possible or useful to reform traditional, incrementalist budgeting practices?*

In order to answer this question, longitudinal case study work was undertaken in two very contrasting English local authorities – Eastmet and Southshire – to examine budget practices before and after the election of the New Labour government in 1997.

The chapter has argued that in the period 1997–2003, UK local/central government relations entered a new phase under a New Labour government. This new phase provided an opportunity to observe the outworking of significant new policy measures which challenge the tradition of incremental budgeting at Eastmet and Southshire.

Arguably, this new phase is a matter of subtleties; and continuities between Conservative and New Labour policies for local government must be acknowledged. Indeed, the 'modernisation' agenda project carried out by New Labour (1997–2003) might be explained as a distinct UK interpretation of the NPM (Olson *et al.*, 1998; Guthrie *et al.*, 2005).[1] In order to establish that the period 1997–2003 represents a new phase in local government political and financial management, Chapter 2 will consider more closely what the New Labour modernisation project and the new policies have meant for authorities like Southshire and Eastmet.

2

Local Government Reform: The New Labour Modernisation Project

Introduction

Paradoxically, local government budgeting and taxation did not have the high media and political profile at the beginning of the project that ultimately emerged at the end of the research period. Although it became an increasingly politically contentious issue (Hetherington, 2004; Hurst, 2004); wider issues concerning the appropriate level of local versus central funding will be dealt with in Chapter 5. The aim of this chapter is to set out the wider regulatory and financial framework within which the case study authorities were operating. The focus will be on the issues that seemed to concern the interviewees, namely central/local financial relations (especially the specific level of central government grant) and the white papers and legislation that characterised the period from 1997 to 2003. The chapter will thereby set out the rules of a budgetary game, which were written in Westminster rather than city or county halls.

The reforms after 1997 are labelled the *modernisation programme* as this seemed to be the predominant mantra of Prime Minister Blair's domestic agenda in the period. The New Public Management (NPM) reforms initiated by the Conservative government (1979–1997) were clearly informed by an understanding of the power of financial management (Bromwich and Lapsley, 1997; Mayston, 1998). In the specific area of local finance, central government power was extended through the nationalisation of the business rate which pushed the proportion of local expenditure covered by local taxation down to about 25 per cent on average and through the caps on increases in council tax. These financial stringencies were accompanied by a policy of Compulsory Competitive Tendering (CCT), beginning with blue collar services in 1988 (such as refuse disposal and street cleaning) and extending later to white collar areas such as legal services, financial services and housing management (Seal, 1999).

One difference that did seems apparent in the 1997–2003 period was that although efficient and effective management was still a primary concern, there was an attempt to modernise the mechanisms of local democracy. With strong tradition of local government activism and influenced by the concepts of the Third Way (Giddens, 1998), the New Labour administration in 1997 began with a commitment to reforming local government rather than constraining as with the previous Conservative government.

Yet residual loyalties did not mean that local government would be given complete license from central government scrutiny and control. Although the new government abolished the much disliked CCT and the capping of local government expenditure, it still retained reserve powers to control local expenditure and required local authorities to deliver services based on the new principles of 'Best Value'. More recently, the Comprehensive Performance Assessment (CPA) extended the inspection of local government from service delivery to issues of corporate performance including areas such as planning, financial management and corporate reporting systems.

With CPA (Audit Commission, 2002) the Audit Commission ranks the corporate performance of authorities rather than just evaluating individual service areas as under the Best Value regime. The significance of the CPA framework and the expanded model of audit is that central government uses the resultant assessment as a basis for rewarding good performance and identifying sub-standard performance. High performing councils were to be allowed greater financial freedoms to spend their budgets as they decided. As will be shown below, the growth of ring-fencing by central government made such freedom much more attractive.

Financial aspects of central/local relations

One of the supreme ironies of the period from 1979 to 1990 was that although her government was content to denigrate and minimise the role of local government, it was a local government issue that contributed to Mrs. Thatcher's downfall. With her insistence, the community charge or 'Poll tax' was introduced as a replacement for 'the rates', a property tax based on notional rental value. However, popular unrest meant that not only was the government forced to abolish the poll tax and introduce the council tax but the associated upheavals led to the replacement of Mrs Thatcher by John Major.

Although the focus of the research has been on the case authorities, with an average of 75 per cent of local revenue coming from central government grants, central–local relations are an important area for every local government chief finance officer. Indeed, the annual announcement of central government grant is a vital input into the local government budgetary cycle. For example, Eastmet's tax and spending choices are driven by a simple equation:

> *The budget* **less** *Formula grant* **equals** *The sum required from council tax.*

The above equation shows that early and accurate prediction of the central government grant is an important input into the budgetary process. The 'formula' terminology implies a technical, objective basis for the grant. Indeed, the grant is nominally based on a needs-based formula which should recognise the special circumstances of each authority in terms of its demographics and other characteristics. However, as problems of steep tax rises and school budget shortfalls during the research project illustrated, both technical failures to estimate costs and political decisions to re-distribute away from southern shire counties (e.g. Southshire) to northern metropolitan authorities (e.g. Eastmet) generated impacts that put several ministerial careers at risk.

Although it is beyond the scope of the research to follow all aspects of central/local financial relations (see e.g. Hale and Capaldi, 2003), the study examined the problem of ring-fencing. The desire for central government control was reflected in an increase in the 'ring-fencing' of local finance to ensure that local authorities met central government priorities for areas such as education. Ring-fenced grants increased from 5 per cent of all Government grant in 1997 to local authorities to 12 per cent in 2001–2002 with a projected 15 per cent by 2003–2004 (DTLR, 2001). Ring-fencing is a crude way to ensure that local units adhere to central priorities by insisting that certain central government grants can only be spent in specified ways.

A senior civil servant interviewed for the study described ring-fencing as follows:

> It's a description of a way in which you give grant ... you've got to spend it on this; you can't spend it on that. The earliest example is the Paupers Lunatic Act 1907. They didn't use the

> word "ring-fencing"! We talk about special and specific grants. Special grants can be ring-fenced or have conditions attached. In recent years ring-fencing has been going up ... So there are more concerns as to what it means.... If an area is a "problem" ... the simplest thing to say is: we'll spend more. From a policy perspective ring-fencing is an easy control. Maybe the place it's needed more is when you can't measure outcomes ...

The last sentence is significant because government clearly believed that it was possible to measure outcomes in the public sector. Moreover, an outcome measurement capability enabled a more exchanged-based system of control such as a Public Sector Agreement (PSA). These principles of trading reward for performance were explained in the White Paper (DTLR, 2001) *Strong Local Leadership, Quality Local Services* in which the government set out a policy that implied greater devolved funding for local authorities in combination with a new performance framework aimed to make ring-fencing less necessary. If the performance setting and inspection regime of Best Value introduced after 1997 was at first only loosely linked to local budgeting, the new mechanisms linked it much more closely. The official explained the logic of linking performance with financial reward as follows:

> My job is to review ring-fencing, asking if we can move from ring-fencing to something based on outcomes.... [With PSAs] ... if you meet all these stretch targets ... then you get an entirely un-ring-fenced reward. We would say this is a good thing in terms of passing control to local government.
>
> ... We're looking for more control for local authorities, and PSAs are a way to go.

By the summer of 2003, the majority of local authorities had either agreed PSAs or were negotiating them. The potential extra funding was estimated to be as much as £1.5 billion with more money on offer in a second round of agreements (LGA, 2004).

The introduction of Best Value

Hood (1995) evokes public sector management in the early twentieth century in his model of perfect public administration (PPA). The picture he portrays is a relatively predictable world with elaborate but clearly defined roles for political representatives and officials. Services were delivered by a 'Jesuitical core' of officials in a high trust, bureaucratic environment. From the PPA perspective, budgeting had a relatively limited role and was legitimated as a way of ensuring basic financial control, ensuring financial probity (by avoiding contamination from the private sector) and adhering to due constitutional process.

The various Conservative policies described through the umbrella term of the NPM (Hood, 1995; Olson *et al.*, 1998) may have resulted in some changes in service delivery through innovations such as compulsory contractualisation but did not necessarily change long established budgetary practices (Walsh, 1995; Seal, 1999). (Although Conservative policies did change schools budgeting practice quite directly; schools were given more power to control their own budgets but also subject to a national curriculum and transparent performance indicators.

The Local Government Act (1999) introduced a duty on the basis of *Best Value* requiring councils 'to deliver services to clear standards covering both cost and quality by the most effective, economic and efficient means available for local people' (DETR, 1998, Chapter 7. p. 1). Under Best Value, local authorities were required to set standards for those services for which they are responsible while for certain services such as education and social services, the government set national standards. Rather than being driven by service providers, the new local government policy agenda was 'starting from cross-cutting problems and issues facing citizens and communities' (Benington *et al.*, 1999, p. 6).

Best Value required the establishment of a 'performance management framework'. This framework was to be composed of a performance plan, an agreed programme of performance reviews, the setting of targets for improved performance, an independent audit of the service reviews and performance targets. The performance framework for Best Value was to involve a hierarchy of indicators. At the apex of the pyramid there would be a small number of nationally standardised 'general health' indicators that would 'reflect the underlying capacity and performance of local authorities as both democratic institutions and bodies responsible for managing a significant share of public expenditure' (DETR, 1998,

Chapter 7, p. 5). The government also set 'key indicators reflecting the effectiveness and quality of local services' (DETR, 1998, Chapter 7, p. 5). Best Value was accompanied by a system of audit and inspection in order to check on information and management systems. The Best Value regime also had a mechanism for intervention in the case of a failing local authority.

From Best Value to CPA

While Best Value evolved over the years, it could be argued that the early emphasis was on non-financial indicators, continuous improvement and a revival of corporate planning. Attempts to link non-financial plans to *financial* planning were somewhat *ad hoc* via mechanisms such as auditors' reports (Audit Commission, 1999). A senior official in the Audit Commission explained the relationship between CCT, Best Value and CPA as follows:

> It (Best Value) was replacing CCT which was very service focused ... it (Best Value) was wider ... a development ... there was a "challenge" element , a "consultation" element ... and following on, "comparing" and "competition". The best councils asked how it fitted in with the priorities overall. ... the Best Value performance plan was supposed to bring it all together.... It's easy to measure more and more and more ... we want to make sure it doesn't burgeon too much. There are the CIPFA indicators. Best Value is the one government really cares about. The CPA targets will come out of these. There are also plans ... about 70 ... the idea is to get that down to half ... we shouldn't be controlling processes and inputs if we can measure these outcomes.

This quotation revealed a fundamental faith in performance measurement which might have surprised earlier researchers on the public sector (see Seal, 2003). This interviewee also saw CPA as a way of strengthening the links between planning, financial management and performance measurement. As he put it:

> The CPA came from the 1999 Audit Commission report ... "Planning to succeed service and financial planning in local government" I think that has a lot of crucial things ... very much the switch towards linking processes ... community strategy ... service planning ... using your finances to support your priorities ... not just book-keeping.

He also explained the philosophy and methodology behind CPA:

> We asked four simple questions....
>
> What do they want to achieve? Their focus – how they focus on that ... how they allocate resources ... budgeting is crucial in that ... its not unlike EFQM ... what's your financial capacity? Your approach to procurement ... and the performance management side ... what have you achieved ... delivered? We looked at improvements in services ... and investments ... the building block for delivery in the future ... like ... disinvestments ... procurement system ... what do you plan to do in the future – are you a learning organisation ... are you addressing weaknesses?

The CPA regime clearly saw the planning role of budgeting as being central to the practice of good local governance. As the Audit Commission official put it:

> Part of the corporate assessment looked at how people prioritised ... Have you used your finance to prioritise? Are you planning ahead? There would be reference to whether people were using their budgeting effectively. Under Best Value, there was no encouragement to prioritise ... the new Best Value regulations don't require all services to be reviewed ... not over a five year period ... it allows them to think about priority services. Or you might want to look for efficiency savings from low priority areas you *have* to do. The CPA should ... help people have a more holistic view.

In the official guides to CPA (Audit Commission, 2002), each of four service themes is given a score between 1 and 4, based on the following scale:

1. *Very weak*: Few or no identifiable strengths.
2. *Fairly weak*: Some strengths, but on balance these are outweighed by weaknesses.
3. *Fairly strong*: Some weaknesses, but on balance these are outweighed by strengths.
4. *Very strong*: Few or no identifiable weaknesses.

The scores for the themes are used to inform an overall judgement on the corporate performance of the authority.

Public/private partnerships

Although CCT had been abolished, the mandatory imposition of contractual governance via outside providers could still take place.

Council services deemed to have failed by inspectors could be taken away from direct local authority provision via some form of public/private partnership (PPP). The implications for budgeting in this instance are quite radical. For example, where local educational management was compulsorily outsourced, as in Eastmet, part of the educational budget that was previously directly managed by the education department was now controlled by private contractors to whom educational expenditure was revenue received in exchange for contractually specified educational outcomes. In capital projects, such as school building, there was also an increased use of partnership arrangements with private contractors informed by Best Value principles and increasingly financed via the Private Finance Initiative (Broadbent and Laughlin, 2005; Pollock, 2004; Shaoul, 2005). Some of these contracts specified open-book accounting and even provisions where cost savings were to be shared between the contractor and local authority. Incrementalism was implicitly challenged by the process of contract specification as fundamental questions about the nature of the service had to be asked and set out in performance criteria.

PPPs were undoubtedly at the heart of New Labour's manifesto commitment to deliver on public services with detailed aspirations being set out by organisations such as the New Local Government Network (Filkin *et al.*, 2001). For local government, a key policy proposal was the aim to bring together different parts of the public sector as well as the private, business, community and voluntary sectors so that different initiatives and services support each other. These ambitious aspirations heralded implications for budgetary practice with the possibilities for both long term financial planning and pooled budgets.

New political/management systems for local government

Local government modernisation in period 1997–2003 has also been associated with increased local engagement (Martin, 1998). Local people were engaged as individual consumers of council services or through neighbourhood- and community-based forums such as neighbourhood panels. The degree of engagement varied from simple information provision through consultation, involvement and delegation (Martin, 1998, p. 7). Prompted by local government Acts, local authorities were also beginning to establish new political and management structures. The old management structures were almost inevitably incrementalist with big departments that were in alliance with specialised council committees. For example, under new structures the old service departments were now called directorates and could be placed in one organisational unit under a Chief Executive of Operations. Other proposals were designed to strengthen the corporate core through the establishment of local government cabinets and directly elected mayors.

Conclusion

This chapter has set out an overview of the regulatory, administrative and financial environment within which the case authorities were managing the budgetary process during the period 1997–2003.

Summarising, there were strands that reveal continuity with earlier Conservative, NPM reforms. CCT had gone but compulsory outsourcing was still seen as an alternative by New Labour if service provision was deemed to be failing. Ideologically, the modernisation programme had the same unquestioning faith in the inherent efficiency of the private sector contracting as was evident with the Conservative era.

The chapter has also identified a number of indirect, but potentially powerful new challenges to incrementalist budgeting. The increasing use of ring-fenced funding by New Labour introduced a new imperative to link local budget priorities to agreed performance targets. Under the CPA, budgeting was newly identified as a core element of good local governance; with the processes for effective budget priorities forming part of an overall corporate assessment rating awarded by external auditors. PPPs, as well compulsory outsourcing of services in the case of failing services, fundamentally challenged incrementalism, with a requirement to scrutinise future service plans and funding and the possibility of pooled budgets. Finally, new political and management structures had the potential to dismantle one of the pillars of incrementalism – traditional service departments allied to inevitably partial council committees.

A further conclusion about the reform programme over the period 1997–2003 was that in some areas the reforms seemed to be codifying some best practice that had already emerged in a number of authorities. For example, Leach and Charteris (2000) describe how a strategic executive structure was adopted by their case study in the early 1990s. This type of structure has now been officially endorsed in legislation. Best Value has also codified the longstanding practice of local authority benchmarking (Bowerman and Ball, 2001).

The next two chapters will describe how officials and members made out within the legislative and inspection framework and the extent to which they could develop distinctive and innovatory budgetary practices.

3

Eastmet

The City of Eastmet Metropolitan District Council was a large council in England, serving a diverse and multi-cultural population of some 500,000 people, and managing an annual revenue budget in excess of £500 million[1] Two-thirds of the area was rural, but the same proportion of the population lived in urban areas, mostly in the city of Eastmet. The area had an ethnically diverse population with almost 20 per cent of the population of Pakistani, Bangladeshi or Indian origin, while about 3 per cent were of Afro-Caribbean or other non-white origin. Unemployment rates were relatively high at nearly 2 per cent above the national average. The average wage was lower than the national average and 44 per cent of children lived in low-income households, compared to 27 per cent nationally.[2]

Embracing the New Public Management: Compulsory competitive tendering and internal charging

Although during the main part of the fieldwork Eastmet was a hung council with a loose Conservative–Liberal Democrat alliance, it had experienced a period of Conservative control when the local party had seen itself as a pioneer of the new business-led model of local government associated with the New Public Management (NPM). Thus rather than dragging its feet, the authority had introduced a system of trading accounts and internal charging irrespective of coercive pressures for the re-organisation of provision in terms of devolved budgets and contractualisation. The philosophy of the internal charging system (ICS) was to 'generate a climate of co-operation and partnership between linked departments to maintain in-house provision of all services in the most efficient and effective way possible on a "preferred supplier of quality services" basis'.[3]

As described in Seal (2003), the imposition of universal rate capping together with other forms of financial stringency forced Eastmet to cope with year after year of budgetary stress. Until 1993, budget reductions were accommodated through budget decrements. In this early phase of cuts, Eastmet applied across-the-board percentage cuts without seriously evaluating the relative merits of departments. As the Chief Finance Officer explained, however, with budgetary stress a more or less permanent feature, the authority moved to a model whereby services were weighted according to political priorities, and different percentage cuts applied to different areas.

The political prioritisation regime began to fail as cuts in some services began to go so deep as to call into question their very existence. Thus even before Best Value, the budgetary regime was pushing the authority towards service review. The traditional lack of focus on outcomes made these reviews potentially *ad hoc*, and Best Value clearly offered a methodology for a more systematic review. Most noteworthy, the authority's budgetary review process could be understood not solely in terms of the expediency of cuts, but linked to a longer-term vision of the local community and the authority's role in shaping that vision. Coinciding with the advent of modernisation, new structures, new management technologies, and political and managerial commitment all came together at the same time.

The modernisation era (I): The impact of new political structures on the practice of budgeting

Eastmet's response to the government's modernisation programme varied in its application. In some areas it was a leader in innovation. For example, it was chosen to pilot a specific project in the early days of Best Value. However, the authority was relatively late in establishing new political structures.

In common with many local authorities, Eastmet introduced a cabinet style of executive. The main feature of the cabinet model was that the old committees based on services such as education, social services and so on, were replaced by a small group of senior members each of them hold a portfolio of responsibilities. The bulk of the members (who all formerly sat on the service committees) became 'backbenchers' sitting on newly formed *scrutiny committees*. The aim of the reform was to strengthen the corporate core of the authority, and to encourage a cross-cutting and more strategic perspective for councils. Management structures and processes were also re-aligned to support the new political structures as shown in Figure 3.1.

The interviewees expressed a variety of views. For example, positive opinions came from the Head of Performance who said that

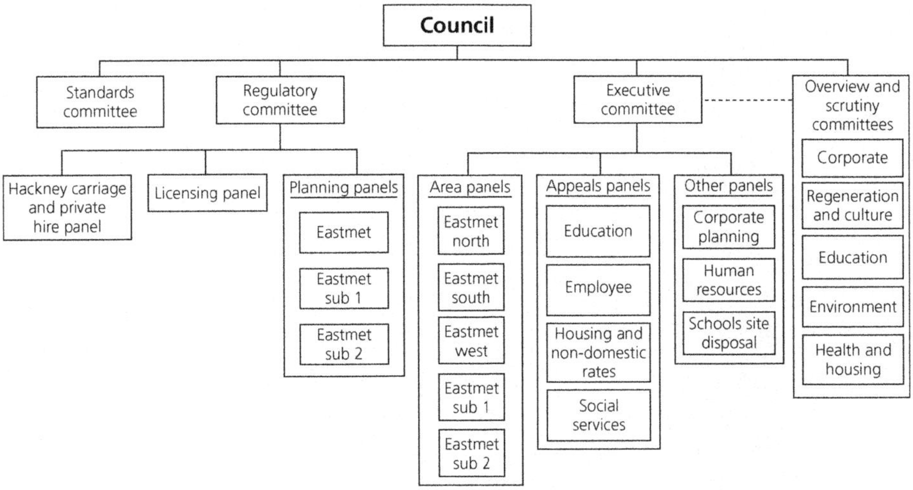

Figure 3.1 The new decision-making structure.

'having portfolios is very helpful especially when things are cross-cutting ... the broader picture is helpful'. In contrast, the deputy council leader was less enthusiastic: 'Utter waste of time and money!' But later in the interview, he said:

> 'What has helped with having a cabinet is that it does break up the silos ...' (with the old service committees) '... you automatically set up going native, advocating their own service ... so it does break that down and make it easier to set priorities ... I feel like the Chancellor of the Exchequer ... telling colleagues "you can't have the money" (or) "we can't put council tax up by 60 per cent"'.

As might be expected, the senior officials were generally more enthusiastic about the new structures. The finance director explained how the model had evolved as follows:

> You've got the 4 portfolio holders – clear governance.... By having the portfolio holders.... It makes it easier to focus on priorities ... The (Old) social services chair wasn't expected to weigh the needs of social services against education ... You have the 4 portfolio holders and their shadows ... But they also own the *corporate* priorities – the executive own *all* of them. There's a shared vision ... The committees are there, but they're there to scrutinise ...

From a member point of view, one clear advantage of the old system was that every elected member could sit on one of the service committees. The finance director accepted that 'there is an issue'. As he explained:

> In a council of 90, 10 out of 90 sit on the executive and many don't sit on the scrutiny committees – they get thrown titbits. There's also a view of the world that it's not the role of 90 members to be on the executive. You are moving towards a parliamentary system ...

The use of terms such as 'cabinet' or 'parliament' actually seemed a little strange in a programme of political modernisation. At national level, cabinet government was in decline, and Whitehall departmentalism was a significant problem. Yet, the new structures did seem to enable a closer alignment between council priorities and budget allocations.

The modernisation era (II): The impact of Best Value, comprehensive performance assessment and performance management

Eastmet was a pioneer of Best Value with several of its senior officials helping to develop the policy after the 1997 election. The authority was awarded a pilot Best Value scheme and was given 'Beacon Status'. At first, Best Value was not really integrated into the budgeting system. For example, officers involved in implementing Best Value argued in the summer of 1999 that Best Value had not yet started to feed through to service deliverers and thus through to budgets. The lack of linkage with budgeting did not stop the authority developing its performance indicators (PIs), a Performance management framework (by December 1999) and publish its first annual Best Value Performance Plan (BVPP) in 2000 (as required by Local Government Act 1999). Best Value was beginning to develop its own routines with monthly monitoring of performance. Elected members and top management began to receive regular reports of performance against targets. Service reviews were undertaken by a team of reviewers taken from relatively senior officials.

The impact of Best Value on budgeting gradually increased as the new reporting systems and PIs bedded down. With spreadsheets of PIs being reported to Chief Executive on an exception basis, a new

Figure 3.2 Eastmet's service delivery process.

reporting system was being developed with monthly reports being fed into an emerging structure of executive and scrutiny committees. Although the newly created Directorates still had their own budgets, there was now an expectation that resources would be moved around as guided by the new performance-planning framework illustrated in Figure 3.2. In contrast with the old departmental committees that were tied to particular services, the scrutiny committees acted more like parliamentary select committees and could only make recommendations. With Lead Members each assigned a portfolio, the aim was to foster a more 'thematic organisation'.

An important change in personnel occurred with the appointment of a new chief executive with a background in the government's Benefits Agency rather than local government. Even without other changes to personnel, a longitudinal comparison in interviews of key senior staff (especially in the finance department) revealed that the prevailing performance and public engagement culture was changing both their language and their actions. For example, an original scepticism with the public consultation process within the finance department had given way to a genuine commitment to align financial plans with articulated local priorities. The articulation of local priorities was channelled in two main ways: the long-standing political processes of elected members and political parties and the more recent mechanism of neighbourhood panels and 'speak-out' forums.

One outcome of the new consultation process was a Community Plan, which set out a number of medium-term priorities for the district. The Plan became the basis for allocating a small investment fund that was created through top slicing. The aim was to allocate the fund to areas consistent with the Community Plan with the understanding that there would be tangible outcomes. As a way of improving an initial lack of linkage between Best Value and budgeting, the authority responded with a new financial strategy based not only on the Community Plan but also on a long-term (twenty year) vision of the authority and the area. Although Eastmet had pioneered its own community planning model, subsequent legislation gave central government support to these local initiatives.

Attitudes to Best Value

Attitudes towards Best Value were mixed, with a number of 'true believers', as might be expected, in the performance management areas. What was striking here was that the usual budgetary methodologies of comparing actual results with targets had become routine and expressed in terms of non-financial as well as financial PIs. As the Performance Director explained:

> 'The council's corporate plan 2002–2005 has corporate priorities ... we have clear goals, say, in relation to social care of vulnerable people. This is an internal working document. We look at goals and when they're supposed to be delivered ... we only have 3 or 5 which aren't going to be delivered ... there are regular (6 monthly) monitoring reports ... So yes, we've got those mechanisms, but we also monitor ... we can look at any PI's linked to this ... pull them out separately in a bi-monthly report. We can look at the quarterly position. If they're in the bottom quartile we can ask people to look at them. People can assess this on-line – service managers can see how their service is performing. The CPA inspector said this is the best (reporting system) they'd seen. So we have monitoring mechanisms as well as – 's [the Finance Director] financial monitoring'.

Examples of how this system works can be seen in Figure 3.3. The document compared actual outcomes with the planned targets in the previous year's Best Value plan. These data were available on

Key performance indicators and targets

Indicator	Actual result 2000/2001	Target for 2001/2002	Actual performance 2001/2002	Sun cloud or lightning	Target 2002/2003	Long term target 2006/2007	Comments on our performance
To increase the resources going into schools	£5 million added to schools budget	To add another £3 million to schools budget	Achieved		To add further £3 million to schools budget	N/a	The objective to add £18 million to schools budget will have been achieved by 2002/2003
Percentage infant classes with more than 30 pupils per teacher	2.3%	0%	0.7%		0%	0%	Some legitimate exceptions push the percentage above 0%
% unauthorised absence: Secondary schools	2.6%	t.t%	2.8%		1.0%	0.8%	Performance was affected by reorganisation but is improving again
GCSE: Percentage with 5 + A′−C grades	32.8%	36.5%	34.3%		39.5%	55%	Results went up but not by as much as hoped. The year group had not come through reorganised schools but through the old system
GCSE: Percentage with t + A′−G grades	91.6%	94.5%	92.3%		97%	99%	Performance on this indicator is sensitive to the absence rate
GCSE: Average points score	30.9	33.5	31.3		36.0	45.0	The average points score did not improve as was hoped
Key Stage 2 Maths: Percentage at Level 4+	58.9%	66%	59.7		73%	98%	Test results improved but not by as much as the targets required. Steady improvement is expected now that the Direct Service Provider is in place
Key Stage 2 English: Percentage at Level 4+	65.9%	72%	68.6		78%	100%	The maths comment applies equally to the English test result
To implement successfully all activities set out in the Ofsted Action Plan	N/a	75%	90%		100%	N/a	Scheduled for completion by August 2002

Figure 3.3 Eastmet performance indicator variances.

the council's website so that Best Value could be seen to enhance public accountability as well as sharpen internal management practices.

Although there was no evidence that anyone actually disliked Best Value, there was some scepticism as to whether it had succeeded in making a difference, especially with respect to the fundamental review process. For example, the Deputy Leader said:

> The problem is I'm still waiting for a Best Value report that says, "Chaps, you don't need to do this". For example, with the introduction of the learning and skills council ... we're not a provider ... we have a legacy because we did the funding before ... so there's a group of staff administering funding ... we've ended up with a whole new function for them providing advice to learning providers....
>
> You keep seeing these BV reviews ... but there's nothing ... no recommendation to outsource ... cease doing ... they favour recommendations which say "put some resources in" ... Elderly services ... the review was excellent... you know, the private sector is dysfunctional ... the diagnosis was fantastic, but the recommendations said "you need to bury more money in it".

Comprehensive performance assessment

In spite of its very real problems in specific service areas, Eastmet came out with the second highest Comprehensive Performance Assessment (CPA) rating. Since many of the deep seated problems of the area can only be explained in terms of global economic and political developments, the council could not be held responsible for poor outcomes. It could, however, try to demonstrate how it was trying to make things better under difficult circumstances. These sentiments seemed to be the sub-text of the Performance Director's comments as follows:

> As a result of the outcome of the CPA there will be an improvement plan. The inspectors expect this – with a limited number of things ... Community safety ... drugs and crime, particularly, it links back to social services and budgets and funding. The cost of new places because of drug abuse is phenomenal. It's about tying some of these things together. The corporate assessment we

> scored highly on – we're good at strategies and plans, and now we need to focus on implementation....We're not necessarily managing ... things across the boundaries. There are also issues around political process ... sometimes we're still a bit old style ...

The finance officials were (at least, initially) more sceptical about CPA. As one official put it:

> The CPA model would work if you had a growth budget and if you have choices, can make decisions about what you spend your money on ... There are limited resources ... CPA identifies areas that are weaker. If the judgement is right, it's a reasonable way of going about your business.

The Finance Director did not believe that the carrot of more financial autonomy would actually be delivered. In later interviews, however, he was much more positive about the way CPA had encouraged a fresh look at some aspects of the finance function. As he put it:

> I could still wax lyrical about some of the banalities of it.... We got our star back on social services, which sorted it.... On the positive side, I can see many more positives ... It has given us a focus ... As a manager, it's given me some specific targets to chase ... in the "use of resources" block, where most of the drivers are...

And once again the Performance Director gave a more upbeat opinion:

> I think if the whole agenda is about improving services for people out there ... then the spirit of it is fine.... You can nit-pick about the methodology and never come to a conclusion about what's right or wrong ... the level of inspection ... PIs ...If the broad framework is broadly right and it helps illuminate to drive things forward ... build capacity ... then its not a bad thing.... There's "challenge" and "support" ... and a need to learn from places who do things well.'

Public service agreements in Eastmet

Public Service Agreements (PSA) were another way in which central government both tried to motivate public service delivery and offer local authorities some autonomy in how they delivered improvements. The Performance Director described Eastmet's approach to PSA as follows:

> We're negotiating now. We need 12 targets – some national ... some local ... to lever the incentive payment down. There need to be stretch targets ... they want to know how you'll use both the (initial) funding and the end money to improve performance. It involves the ODPM [Office of the Deputy Prime Minister] and the DFES [Department for Education and Skills] ... The money comes from the ODPM. It's pump priming. For Eastmet it is about £1.25 m. You can get a performance improvement bonus.... A bonus for having met the stretch targets. Probably, for each target, about £1 m, ... about £12 m in total. It's not vast, but it's worth having.

The modernisation era (III): The impact of public/private partnerships on the practice of budgeting

As explained in Chapter 2, the change of government in 1997 was expected to see a reduction in the use of contractual governance in the public sector. But although competitive tendering was no longer compulsory, New Labour showed a similar enthusiasm to the previous Conservative administration for public/private partnerships. Indeed, it has been an even more enthusiastic proponent of the Private Finance Initiative (PFI) (Pollock, 2004). The most important public/private partnership in Eastmet was in educational management where a highly critical report by the inspectorate led to the compulsory outsourcing of educational management to a private contractor (Education Eastmet).

From a budgeting perspective, there were a number of implications. First, the authority effectively fixed a part of its educational budget for the next ten years. The loss of flexibility was compensated by a transfer of risk to the contractor as the budget had been plagued by perennial overspends. Even more significantly, the contractor's profit depended partly on the achievement of a set of carefully specified and quite demanding PIs. The targets for educational attainment would require a quite substantial improvement in Eastmet's relative position in the national educational league tables as well as improvements in the attainment of specified ethnic and gender groupings.

Attitudes towards the educational contract

One immediate problem for the council was that although they remained in overall charge of educational budgeting, they lost much financial expertise to the contractor (Education Eastmet). As a leading finance official put it:

> The Education accountants went to Education Eastmet. We lost the Education accounting expertise. We had potentially a huge hole had it not been for Jim [an assumed name].

Another development which affected education but was independent of the contractual arrangements was that so much education spending was both formula-driven and controlled by central government. As the finance director put it:

> The biggest single outside impact is more and more targeted resource. It's the highest ever level this year as a proportion of the total grant – about 14 per cent is formally ring-fenced. Over £50 m. It goes against everything the government has said.... The DFES is the killer. They're the biggest culprits. They're no better than the Departments here.... We've never had less freedom to set our own budget. In Education ... a pack of Rottweilers are after you if you haven't spent the money on education. We didn't have an option on half our budget.

As explained in Chapter 1, it was possible to get excellent access to many aspects of the financial management of education in Eastmet. Jim, the senior manager who represented the client (i.e. Eastmet), explained the division of responsibilities as follows:

> Obviously all the budget is Eastmet's responsibility. It's operated through me and the other accountants who work for – [the Director of Finance]. The budget's still the same, but now £26 million goes to pay Education Eastmet. The ... schools' delegated money is still the responsibility of the Director of Education and the Council. But the front line and support of schools, etc., has been maintained by Education Eastmet.

Jim explained the management of the contract as follows:

> £25 million is fixed in the contract, indexed for inflation. That's the agreed contract sum. It allows for variations – statute and

government policy might change and the contract has to be capable of dealing with it. It might end up as a cost to the Council – like this year there's changes to the education of children suspended from school ... now they have to be educated from the next day ... Education [Eastmet] will say that they have to change the level of service ... and it will cost you, [Eastmet] X amount. The contract is managed in a tripartite way. The Director of Education is the "client". He's got all the statutory responsibility. The contractor does some of it and he [the Director of Education] still has about 20 staff. Half of those are Education experts.'

Problems with the educational management contract

During the observation period the contract ran into problems as educational targets were missed. The financial impact of these failures was that bonuses were not paid to the contractor. More controversially, the council agreed to pay the contractor some extra monies which were attributed to contractual variations. These extra payments did not go down well with the school heads as the following exchange from a meeting of the Schools Financial Strategy Group shows:

Head Teacher I (addressing the contractor's representative): The big issue on your paper, though is contract variation ... failed targets ... the £1m... but we're not debating that... we don't know those variations for commercial reasons.

Jim [Education client side]: The £1m... would be an adjustment ... from 2003/04 and onwards.... The contract variations, also have implications for the 18 months of the contact already past ... like excluded pupils ... if that were to be agreed, there'd be a cost to the council in this year as well.

Head Teacher I : So ---- (the contractor) got a contract, they didn't reach the targets ... so it went into a reserve... who's going to get that?... its not going to us in the schools, but we've paid for it through the SEN [Special Educational Needs]!

Head Teacher II: They've got the whole process upside down.

Head Teacher I: So you didn't meet the targets but you're getting another £1m?... Are the council likely to agree to this?

Education Eastmet [contractor]: ... with any contract ... there will be areas ... where the contractor will say there are things we're doing which aren't covered.

Head Teacher II (chuntering): No one gives me another £1m ... to sort things out.

The modernisation era (IV): The impact of cross-service programmes on budgeting practice

Although the council were pioneers in developing cross-service programmes, there was little evidence for pooled budgets. There were, however, a number of cross-cutting projects that could have attracted special funding such as the Neighbourhood Renewal Fund especially in the areas. For example, the finance director explained Eastmet's approach as follows:

> Eastmet is strong on joint working, particularly the NHS [National Health Service] ... police and probation services and to a lesser degree, voluntary services ... There's a partnership commitment, which means a good degree of joined up-ness. I'm spearheading a national project with the Office of the Deputy Prime Minister, looking at using IT and a model for its use around Elderly Social Care – joining up agencies, linking up existing databases ... Age Concern, Health and Social Services, Housing Associations, the NHS... We're looking to draw out some serious money to support it. Our financial problems arise because we're a victim of our own success ...

Budgetary problems at Eastmet (I): the schools funding fiasco

In contrast to Southshire (discussed further in Chapter 4), Eastmet was not hit quite as dramatically with the schools funding crisis of spring 2003. Partly, they were beneficiaries of the general re-distribution of central government support from southern to northern authorities. In addition, the authority did not experience the same degree of incremental drift in teachers' salaries as in Southshire. Finally, they already had a number of schools in deficit so were more used to dealing with budgetary shortfalls in schools.

The main complaint in Eastmet was that the authority had lost a promised extra £11 m from central government as a result of the latter's 'damping' policy. As Eastmet's educational accountant explained:

> ... we had an additional £11 m but then the government damped it down ... the whole formula review was seen as a process of re-distribution of resources from the south to the north ... so

> when we got our formula settlement it was X minus £11 m. In terms of damping ... it's a concern of the whole council – its money we've been told to spend, but haven't been given ...

In addition, he argued that 'the whole machinations of Central Government finance are complex', making it difficult for the officials to explain to the local educational stakeholders why they were not getting the extra funding that they were expecting. The accountant did not see the solution to future funding as lying in more participation from the schools. Rather he argued:

> Maybe the DFES should just cut out the LEA [Local Education Authority] and tell us the budget they're setting for each school block, which is a rebellious concept ...

Paradoxically, leaks from the Prime Minister's office suggested that a version of the Eastmet accountant's 'rebellious concept' was under consideration by members of Tony Blair's think tank. Of course, if schools funding were to be effectively nationalised, local authorities would lose a huge chunk of their overall service responsibility and associated financial issues. When pressed, the accountant admitted that the technical difficulties of such a change were huge because of the 'complexity of setting a useful formula for 30,000 sets of circumstances – the DFES [Department for Education and Skills] can't model each school or each LEA's circumstances'. Given the calculative errors actually made by the DFES (House of Commons Education and Skills Committee, 2003; Audit Commission, 2004), such scepticism as to the Department's technical capacity seemed well founded!

Budgetary problems at Eastmet (I): The social service overspend

While schools funding received much national media coverage, from a budgeting point of view, the problem service area for Eastmet was in social services, especially children's services. The problems, some proposed solutions and the interplay between politics and new systems such as CPA were set out by the Financial

Information Services Manager responsible for social care as follows:

> From a Social Service department overview, there's a potential £1m overspend – we could absorb any level of council tax increase you care to name.... That's clear ... if we don't get the number of children looked after down.... A KPMG report will say we need to fund a prevention service – that is the plan. Council may choose not to go with that – I can't see how they can't, with the financial implications if they don't do it. The social service 3-year plan is demanding about £5m over the next two years, it's fair, but unlikely. Now they're trying to link it into the ... CPA ... and the inspection ... but there's an issue about how much resources are available. It's less easy for a 2 star department to say they need less resources.

The finance manager explained how difficult it was to maintain budgetary control in the post-Lamming[4] climate:

> The overspend is the main financial issue facing the council. If you're spending money on looked-after children, it shows the limitations of what you can do. Finance people don't sit on child protection teams saying you don't have money to do stuff. Then there's Lamming ... but the KPMG report is raising issues about our children's services. It's not a financial document, but its about ... assessment processes, preventative services. If they're out there, children end up being looked after.

The manager explained the unpredictability of budgeting without knowing what the demand might be:

> The 3- year strategy was based on the rising number (20) of looked after children. We added to foster fees – we pay them by far the most in [the County]. £800K was the increase for the year, £400K for the half year. It's been successful – but we've had an increase of 60 children – there are (800) children in looked-after care. Other authorities had been expecting growth – but not like ours.

Indeed, the emotional and ethical issues of trying to exert financial discipline were put very starkly:

> It would be like sitting on a child protection team. ... I'd be unhappy and I can't see it happening. For any other service (like a recreation centre) we'd close it down. The finance director would go in with chains and lock the door. If there are 800 children in the system, that's 800 serious decisions.

The inherent but under-played drama of the budget discussions was evident, as he remarked drolly:

> Given that we've got a £4m overspend, things are pretty calm in here. It's being discussed at Executive Committee in 3 or 4 minutes (!!!!)

Emerging innovations in financial management at Eastmet

Priority-led budgeting

As the above example illustrates, innovations in particular service areas were largely a matter of taking an 'investment' view of cost savings (i.e. spend now to save more in the future). Such an approach was encouraged by the medium term and strategic thinking fostered by senior managers, which meant that by the end of the research period, 'priority-led budgeting' was well established. Both the corporate centre and service managers took a three-year budget view and the criteria for moving resources around were now more clearly linked to local consultation processes. In addition to mechanisms such as neighbourhood panels, there was officer support for each major political grouping. Although shifting political fortunes meant that short-term political expediency might conflict with the longer-term plans, the key change was that budgets could now more readily respond to priorities rather than simply roll over.

Base budget review

In the last visit to Eastmet, the Finance Director was very upbeat about how the budgeting system was evolving. As he put it:

> ... We've been evolving while you've been looking at us.... The story is becoming like Harry Potter ... We're moving very quickly to something quite different.... The thing that's becoming embedded is the idea of corporate priorities as the driver, not service needs.
>
> Cross-Cutting [services] ... are becoming a manifestation...of the corporate priorities being embedded ... In budget-setting, we're asking: What have you (Senior Officers) got to contribute to corporate priorities? The next stage is ... base-budget review and starting to dismantle budgets ... asking what matters to us – the corporate priorities.

The Finance Director explained the difference between zero base budgeting (ZBB) and base budget review (BBR) as follows:

> ZBB is "let's start with nothing" ... BBR looks at the budget we have, and going through on a line-by-line basis ... "Do we need that line, and do we need that much money" (It's) not a green-field site ... You can't just stop and start service provision ... For operational and HR reasons ... You can't pretend things don't exist.... And if we are going to stop things, when? In twelve month's time? We can't pretend we haven't got commitments.

He explained BBR as being consistent with Best Value, but not a consequence of it:

> It's come from 2 sources. One is the recognition that if we have aspirations to spend additional resources on things, we have to stop spending money on other things. The last 12 months debate on council tax increase nationally has shown that. You can't just go on increasing aggregate spend. The other place it comes down from is the corporate priorities agenda – spending more money on those priorities. You should have other clear non-priorities....

BBR involves new levels of participation in the budget process:

> It has to be done in conjunction with budget holders because you can't ignore service knowledge. But we haven't done one yet – it's something to take forward in the next three years.

He explained that there were issues of timing and political commitment. On political obstacles, he said:

> Politically it's difficult to get them [elected members] to commit to it. It takes away their ability to play games with council tax – the opposition always propose higher levels of spending with lower council tax....

The finance director argued that timing was important as if it was undertaken early enough in the budgetary cycle then a more rational dialogue could be established than the traditional 'shroud-waving model' that was typical of old style local government budgetary debates. He pointed out that:

> ... The time to do it is April/May so you (can) make savings ... create capacity to take into the budget process ...

His plan was to introduce BBR to one or two service areas at a time. In Eastmet, the obvious starting point was social services as it was both overspent and had a programme of new projects.

Centralisation of finance function

One of the side effects of the new corporate structure was a centralisation of the finance function by taking finance personnel out of the service areas. The Finance Director explained the significance of this re-configuration of finance as follows:

> Last year the whole Financial Services Department was pulled together. The Social Services Finance Section is, theoretically at least, no longer.... No financial staff are line managed by anyone in a service. They all work for Finance ... its still a work-in-progress ... it's about changing culture. Half the Finance function are people who spent their careers working in Departments. A lot of the Directors are used to having their own Finance Section. The Directors were using their Finance Section to lobby against the Corporate interest. That's what happens. It still happens to an extent. We're trying to change that thinking.

Conclusions

One of the advantages of the longitudinal research methodology is that the research can document how individuals can change both their roles and their attitudes. The involvement in Eastmet had predated the start of the project, making it possible to trace how the finance function had become far more involved with enabling and shaping council policy. The disconnection between the monitoring of the delivery of council services in the early days of Best Value had gone and Best Value was now more related to corporate priorities and the development and implementation of budget policy.

4

Southshire

Southshire was generally very affluent, with a population of around 1 million and was located in the South of England. Although Southshire was the most urbanised shire county in England, 85 per cent of its area was countryside. Ethnic communities comprised less than 3 per cent of the population. Southshire had with virtually no unemployment with significant labour and skills shortages in many areas particularly in technical and support service areas. The annual revenue budget was about £900 million.

In earlier fieldwork, one senior manager described Southshire as 'the California of Britain...a very comfortable place to be...'. Southshire could be viewed as part of a tradition of County government, which 'is about the continuity of an established way of life, a sense of county background' (Stewart, 2000, p. 15). Although the County was Conservative controlled, the dominant political consensus was around pre-Thatcher paternalistic Conservatism, characterised by a belief in welfare, and a duty to provide educational and social services to deserving local families (Chandler, 2001, p. 189). As one Executive Member put it in the course of this study:

> [The County] is terribly affluent but there are pockets of deprivation which makes it worse if you're in that cycle. There is a spiral of decline. We can do something about that ...

And similarly, from the Leader of Southshire Council:

> We want Southshire to be a place which continues to be an attractive place to live and work in... schools where people can achieve their potential... a safety net for the vulnerable... we want the economy to grow, without damaging the environment... we want the roads to be safer.

Chandler (2001, p. 189) suggests that councils like Southshire govern with 'a light paternalistic hand', deferring to Officer (i.e. management) or professional judgement or established professional practices in matters of policy. Arguably, Best Value and other 1997–2003 reform measures might have been absorbed in a way which allowed them to be de-coupled from incrementalist budgeting traditions and practices. Senior managers described how they sometimes had to sell, cajole or re-brand particular New Labour reforms to Conservative Members at Southshire. Members avoided the term 'social inclusion' for example, and preferred to think in terms of an agenda of 'self-reliance'. Members at Southshire, however, seemed willing to commit to the implementation of New Labour legislation in the context of defending the democratic character of local government, and providing local responsive services. For example an Internal Change Consultant employed at Southshire commented:

> ... we knew there was a political modernization agenda crashing over the horizon... we knew there would be an issue ... keeping Members on board... Best Value came along and we could piggy-back... we were going in that way... government embraced what local authorities were doing... we didn't refuse to play ball... we said: well done Labour, you've caught up with us!

From the Conservative to the modernisation era in Southshire

Southshire had been beset by departmentalism (with departments described by one Executive Member as 'huge silos [operating] ... to the detriment of the customer'). There had been a centralised approach to budgeting, supported by departmental finance functions which were established in the early 1990s. Members had traditionally relied on officer judgement to set out basic budget parameters and to put forward suggestions for Council Tax rises. The process had been incrementalist, with the Director of Finance providing a 'rolled-over' budget comprising 'headline' figures. This budget-making process had traditionally been carried out outside the corporate planning process, and was recognised as falling short of expectations. As one Executive Member of Southshire Council explained:

> The budget is rolled-over. [The Director of Finance] comes in with a report... the State of the Nation... Government Headlines... Ball park figures... It's rolled over with 3 per cent inflation ... I would challenge this and I have done for years, this roll-forward process...

There had been little Member involvement in budget-making, but the Leader of the Council took on a central role. One Executive Member described how the 'bulk' of political budget scrutiny was carried out by the 'the Leader... who has taken it upon himself to have the final say...'. Comments included the following from an Executive Member:

> The culture and the Member culture is such that...with the complication of local government funding... we've let him [the Leader] get on with it.

Given the Leader's grip on budget-making, the pre-1997 committee system was described as meeting to 'rubber stamp' budget proposals, with little attempt on the part of Members to interrogate budgets. At the same time, the Council's financial and information systems were generally perceived as having been inadequate for providing the basis of disaggregated service information for better budget-making linked to corporate priorities. For example, the Director of Performance and Resources commented:

> Current processes are focused on assessing with Members whether they want to change current volumes of service...

Similarly, the Head of Finance (Adults and Community Care) suggested that:

> The biggest issue we have is about information. At the moment we have an entirely separate system from the services management system. The planning problem is tying financial information to service information. Depending on which system you look at, we look after 7 or 111/2 thousand older people, which makes tying a budget to a service impossible.

There were similar comments from other service and financial managers, including the following from the Head of Education Finance (I)[1]:

> ... one of the deficiencies here is the accounting system and allied to this the HRM system is poor. There's never been integration. There is scope to be more efficient and effective... There's a lot of human resource working around the system to get the information you want.

Pressures to reform the budget process were building at Southshire before the 1997–2003 modernisation era and these pressures have worked in tandem with the modernisation process. In 1997, the Council had instigated its own series of 'fundamental reviews' (which pre-date Best Value, in spite of the confusing terminology) carried out by around 40 task groups. The aim had been to look for fundamental change in how services were provided and the resources committed to them. In common with Eastmet, these reforming initiatives were driven by budgetary stringency experienced by Southshire. The perception of the Director of Performance and Resources was that Southshire had experienced budgetary pressures throughout the 1990s, but that 1997 brought about increased pressures as a hung Council spent Southshire reserves. The fundamental reviews led to 're-focusing' and achieved a reduction in total spending of around 4–5 per cent of the total Council revenue budget. Since 1997, Central Government requirements to achieve efficiency savings had resulted in Council Tax rises. As the Director of Performance and Resources put it:

> We find a tax level that's acceptable and fit services to it.

Southshire therefore faced different but comparable resource management challenges to those experienced at Eastmet. Southshire, for example, regarded itself as penalised under the government grant system 'for being an affluent area'. During the fieldwork Southshire Members (particularly the Leader) were lobbying the Government to take account of perceived difficulties in providing quality services in a high cost area. Southshire Members were concerned about pressures to increase Council Tax bills as Government transferred local government funding from the South East to the North and Midlands. Southshire had also been implementing a major corporate change programme, 'People First', to develop stronger links between finance and performance in recognition that the corporate planning process was decoupled from the budget-making process.

The modernisation era in Southshire (I): The impact of new political structures on the practice of budgeting

Under a new political structure, Southshire Council was delegating the management of its business to a single party Executive of 10 members, each with responsibility for a specific area of work or 'portfolio'. The Executive has the following portfolios:

- Adults and Community Care
- Best Value and Resources
- Children and Young People
- Communities and Countryside
- Corporate Planning
- Environment
- Investors in People

◆ Public Safety
◆ Transport and the Economy.

Budget scrutiny had become the responsibility of a very small number of Executive portfolio holders. As the Head of Education Finance (I) noted, just one council member (Executive Member, Children and Young People) was consulted about changes in the education budget. The indications from some Officers at Southshire were that the lack of a political scrutiny process had left a 'gap' in respect of decision-making. As the Head of Finance – Adults and Community Care commented, for example:

> [The Assistant Director of Finance] ... gets frustrated as the Services write reports, which get shared with Executive Members ... to get their support for bids [for resources during budget-making] ... Before, these would have gone through service committees – where's the impact? There isn't enough filtering, the committee would have dissected the bids and identified key issues for Council... This year merits quite a lot of focus... We already have a paper saying that we needed £40 m extra to have a sustainable budget... the Executive for Adults and Community Care ... gulped a bit, but became part of the bidding process... Council ... ended up with some very big numbers, which didn't help them very much... There is no filtering process to say what are the things that we can't deal with...

Whilst some Members had viewed the traditional committees' scrutiny role as 'rubber stamping', from an Officer perspective committee member involvement was important in developing a detailed understanding of political support for spending proposals and cuts. The Head of Finance (Adults and Community Care) took the view that spending decisions that had previously been the responsibility of elected Members in service committees with detailed knowledge of service issues would now be devolved to Officers. Similarly, the Deputy Director of Education commented:

> ... now there's only one person who understands Education. Things go through rather more easily. Get your Chairperson on side, and you can do what you like... does anyone believe we have cabinet government ... in this country?

The routine for Executive Member scrutiny of the budget had yet to fully develop. Further, the role of the select committees in budget-making at Southshire had yet to be determined. As the Executive Director, Performance and Resources put it:

> The big problem is that you're limited to 10 people on the Executive... what do you do with the other 67 [Members]? ... we're re-organising it ... the scrutiny function is only a small part of the structure we've created... yes we do miss the committees... the level of support

An Internal Change Consultant also took the view that there was 'a need for the skills base [to be] reestablished in select committees.'

The Leader continued to take a central role in budget-making, however. As he put it:

> Not many Members have got to grips with the scrutiny role... I do more scrutiny of the budget than they do... they do come up with some nice ideas, but if you were to ask, how are you going to cut £5 m... they would ask me.

Similarly, an Internal Change Consultant commented:

> [the Leader] takes overall responsibility for Finance. He's absolutely focused on Finance.

However, Southshire was beginning to implement an initiative to establish local Member committees within district boundaries to scrutinise financial resource use in the context of local service outcomes. These local committees were planned to have control of a devolved budget in the order of £40 million.

The modernisation era in Southshire (II): The impact of Best Value and the Comprehensive Performance Assessment

Officials and members frequently claimed that much of the modernisation programme, and particularly Best Value, was simply a codification of some good practices, which managers in Southshire had already implemented. For example the Deputy Director of Education stated:

> Best Value is just a name for things good management should be doing... it is how things should be ... or you could just keep accumulating staff ... before 1997 there was a fundamental

> review by the council... it was a model for Best Value... why do we have an Educational Psychology Service and so on...

Rather than finding any resistance to the principles behind Best Value, there was evidence of scepticism about its impact 'on the ground'. The Head of Finance (Adults and Community Care) commented that:

> Best Value has hardly impinged on what we do as a service. It's something that happens corporately. Chief Officers and Members get very excited by it.... It's a hoop you have to jump through.

The indications were that Officers in both the Education and Social Services were rather more concerned with maintaining the political support of (respectively) Department for Education and Skills (DFES) officials ('We have to keep an eye on that relationship... the funding streams might be affected') and working towards improvement in relation to the schools' and social services inspectorates.

As was evident in Eastmet, Best Value did not begin with a financial focus. As the Adult and Community Care finance officer continued:

> We've had two or maybe three Best Value reviews that relate to Social Care. There wasn't a single £ sign in them, no references to money... the Social Services Inspectorate are far more interested in things like how well individual care files are maintained, key workers being allocated to children in need.

The impact of the CPA

The Comprehensive Performance Assessment (CPA) seemed to have had greater political impact at Southshire than Best Value, with attendant impacts on the budgetary process. The increased emphasis on Central Government's performance management agenda was reflected in an enhanced role for the Director of Finance, who assumed the title of Director of Performance and Resources at the beginning of 2002. He explained his role in the following terms;

> My role is ensuring that the performance management framework is okay and responding to the CPA. There may be financial freedoms and flexibilities – we are working with everyone on that.

In common with Eastmet, Southshire was rated 'good' in the first round of CPA assessments. Characteristically seeing itself as a soundly-managed authority, Southshire volunteered itself as a pilot for the CPA process (it was previously a Best Value pilot site). Social care had not been a political priority in the authority, and the authority has used tighter criteria on eligibility on social care to 'rein back' spending in the context of ongoing budgetary pressure. The 'good' rather than hoped for 'excellent' rating on the first CPA assessment, however, led to a political decision in 2002 to increase Council Tax by 11.4 per cent to provide additional funding in this area. The Executive Director, Performance and Resources commented that:

> The organisation's objective, driven by the Leader, is to be the best local authority in England... we were only 'good' in the CPA – we weren't 'good' in social care... one star rather than two star... So we weren't 'excellent' ... we want to be the community leader rather than just setting the Council Tax.... The ... inspectorates would say you got one star because you didn't spend the money ... CPA has been taken seriously...viewed as a judgement on the Chief Executive and the Leader... If you're Arsenal, you expect to win the League.

Southshire's People First initiative was seen as pre-empting financial and performance management requirements under the CPA. As the Director of Performance and Resources put it:

> The CPA happened at a time when we were planning to do the things we're actually doing (May, 2003)

Other interviewees noted that the Audit Commission recruits from local authorities, including Southshire. The Deputy Director of Education commented, '...our top performance person has gone to the Audit Commission... he's taking things with him... it's a two-way process.'

In May 2003 the Director of Performance and Resources explained that his job title had changed again (to Executive Director, Performance and Resources); and explained how People First was intended to build capacity in performance management. Problems with effective service delivery, partially uncovered by the Best Value review process, led to concerns that the budget process should be focused at 'lower levels' than the traditional departmental bases. As the Head of Education Finance (I) noted, 'People First is about trying to get away from the old Departments.' Individuals at service (sometimes referred to as 'business') level were identified who were prepared to take on 'financial, service and cultural control' (Executive Member). A new mechanism, 'Service Commissioning Agreements', aimed to set up around 30 agreements with Southshire Heads of Service to incorporate outcome targets as well as budgets. The Director of Performance and Resources explained the progress of these arrangements (March, 2002):

> They won't be that good this year as there are new people... the key task is then to use these as the basis of next year's business plan. We want to start in April/May ... asking... where would services like to go and consult Members and ensure proper resourcing...

Similarly, the Internal Change Consultant explained the intentions of the Service Commissioning Agreements:

> Each Head of Service has to produce their own ... contract with the strategy team... I guess its largely on an exception basis ... if you're not achieving targets, why? And do we need to change them... It started April last year ... and there's much clearer individual responsibility...

Social care was seen as a key area in which to implement the new system of budgetary and performance control. The Service Commissioning Agreements were seen as an attempt to break the link between spending on social care and *ad hoc* Member decisions in response to constituent appeals and pressures ('it should be politicians who say no to people', Executive Director, Performance and Resources).

The People First policy entailed the restructuring of the old Southshire Departments. Schools support services became a unified service operating on the basis of functionally mixed teams within different areas of Southshire. Traditional boundaries between the two major service silos (and traditional political power bases) of Education and Social Services were eroded. The old 'Special Educational Needs' section was married with Social Services to create a unified Children's Service. The eventual outcome was to be merged budgets. These changes were generally viewed as important, particularly in overcoming barriers to effective working between different professional groups in Education and Social Services.

Southshire had made significant investments in its budgetary and performance system. The People First initiative had been supported by a consultancy firm and by an Internal Change Consultant employed permanently at Southshire. Further significant investment in an ERP (Enterprise Resource Planning) system were planned to provide information at service level, which was previously unavailable. The Internal Change Consultant took the view that:

> If you're going to make that shift, you need those [ERP] systems. You need to release finance to the front line. The financial system is on its knees – so we're going down the ERP route.

Similarly the Executive Director, Performance and Resources explained that:

> Our IT 2½ years ago was the worst of out support services... we took decisions to invest... ERP is designed to replace financial systems, but also the business processes, like recruiting people. We'll do this ruthlessly and the investment will pay for itself...

These changes were informed by changing perceptions about services, service users in the County and the need to understand better how to link resources to their needs. All of these pressures were being felt at the time the CPA was being introduced. An Executive Member suggested that:

> Most people are becoming more demanding of a whole set of things... the whole 'E' thing is driving a set of aspirations. Some of it is coming from over the pond and going down the courts route ... if you don't get your kids into the right school. Swimming pools ... people want an experience not the old verruca one... We have one million customers (there are customers who come into the County) so the relationship between their expectations and what their needs are ... there has to be some assessment of that and balancing... we can't do it all, we need to know what it is to be a good provider.

There were similar comments from service managers, including the following from the Head of Psychology and Assessment:

> ... in any part of [Southshire] there are very young children from 0 or 6 months with development difficulties.... The professional group in the LEA ... pick up those referrals... We are completely unable to control this, but we have a certain capacity. It's a constant pressure to expand because of better pre-natal care and post-natal care is so much better than it used to be. There's huge

emphasis on us getting much more involved much earlier... It's driven ... also by the parents here [in Southshire] who are very well informed.

And the following from the Deputy Director of Education:

> The budgets were running away and there were huge budget tussles... some [local authority looked-after] children cost £100K per year... It was pass the parcel, not arrangements... we can do better...

The modernisation era in Southshire (III): The impact of public/private partnerships and cross-cutting issues on the practice of budgeting

Pre-1997 Compulsory Competitive Tendering (CCT) arrangements were viewed by interviewees at Southshire as having played a part in the wider agenda for value-for-money in local services. The Director of Performance and Resources commented, for example:

> CCT was effective in wiping out the worst excesses of local government ... especially refuse collection and housing maintenance... nothing was ever value for money... it was appalling.

CCT was not viewed as 'very engaging', however. Generally Southshire Members were not ideologically committed to CCT. Although one Executive Member recognised that 'you could outsource the whole lot' of local government services, outsourcing on ideological grounds ran counter to political commitment to services run by a locally elected Southshire Council.

For reasons better described as pragmatic rather than ideological, therefore, the Council made increasing use of the Private Finance Initiative (PFI) to finance changes in services or new service areas. Linked to a fundamental review, the PFI had been used to finance elderly persons homes; in response to a changing Central Government agenda for waste management (Ball *et al.*, 2006); and to Southshire's own agenda for improving arrangements for school transport through a school bus service ('a fleet of badge-branded coaches'). The PFI had also been used to re-launch failing schools. As the Head of Education Finance (II) explained:

> We tend to close [failing schools] and re-launch them. For particular bad schools you can get government funding, but we don't

always trigger funding. We can't keep putting money into failing schools... one failing schools was closed and re-launched with a private partner... it's like walking into a hotel, with internet cafes ... There is an impact.

The modernisation era (IV): The impact of cross-service programmes on budgeting practice

In Southshire, organisational changes had *anticipated* modernisation philosophies of cross-cutting by creating an integrated children's service which combined the traditional Local Education Authority (LEA) and community services. The Head of Children's social services explained his role as follows:

> I manage all the children services .... The education side ... and adoption, permanency and fostering .... Children through to adults at 21 .... I'm very diverse. I came here June 1997.... In 1996/7, the reshaped department was created (with) a children's services branch running all the support services (for schools).... I was head of that. Social Services had the same sort of branch – in social care. Both branches were established in 1997. Both Heads thought we should be one service.... There's a massive overlap between social services and education for children with special needs. We saw it was important .... The fundamental review looked at work on a thematic basis. ... these children are on a continuum ... not just an education or social care problem...

The Head of Social Services took the view that central government was not as joined up or as modernised as local government:

> The DFES [Department for Education and Skills] thinks mechanically ... only one ward [local area] met the criteria for targeted funding for the NNI (Neighbourhood Nursery Initiative). [This ward] has our highest concentration of people from a Bangladesh and Pakistan backgrounds ... one thing that they don't need is wrap-around childcare. They don't trust the state – they have the extended family. But they listened – the DFES... are going to have to listen much more – get out of this mechanistic way ... formulae ... There has been flexibility in responding to local need. They are getting there.

With children's social services linked to education, Adult and Community Services (ACS) were left as a free-standing area within the council. However, here, the main cross-cutting initiative was with the National Health Service (NHS) which wanted to free up beds occupied by old people who required beds because of a lack of alternative care rather than for acute medical reasons – the so-called 'bed-blockers'. The Chief Finance Officer in ACS was beginning to grapple with these organisational and budgetary issues. As he described it:

> We've changed all our boundaries to 5 geographical areas which are co-terminus with the PCTs [Primary Care Trusts] in Surrey in response to Social Care and Health working together, or being abolished. The horrors of transition would last 5 years! We're looking at services merging ... pooled budgets.
>
> One of the issues is that we're separately organised, we have separate statutory responsibilities, separate... we don't treat people's needs holistically. We don't ask how they are treated appropriately. The system ... the new PCTs are beginning to admit this ...that there is inappropriate administration ......they deteriorate ...they end up at the output end, and they've lost independence ......we're then paying for people for the rest of their lives. But we only use the money if it's about lifetime funding. So we end up with a commitment, but no funding.
>
> We can only agree to take them on if there's funding. It dents bed-blocking numbers ... but then the beds are refilled. "Cash for change" is supposed to encourage a change in systems of care pathways, putting in support for people in own homes ... Health will have much more of an idea. Its all right saying that ... but they don't accept that there'll still be blocked beds [in the meantime]. We have to say that if you want the numbers down now – we'll have to use the money to get people into care now. The money is only guaranteed for one year. I have to tell people they can't commit money.

Budgetary problems in Southshire (I): The schools funding fiasco

In Southshire, the outturn in 2003 was such that every single secondary school in Southshire had a deficit budget. This problem hit Southshire particularly hard. In part this was because, in contrast to Eastmet, schools were not used to have financial problems.

How, then, had the problem come about in an authority that had a long tradition of efficient educational management?

From a general perspective, the authority was precisely the type of southern shire authority that experienced the combination of unexpected cost pressures and inadequate central government funding. More specifically, the chief of educational finance explained that the usual principle applied to the schools budget was that 'what you got last year plus inflation'. She went on to say:

> The National Insurance increase was expected and built into the budgets but we were caught out by the salary increases- the problem of "incremental drift". There are now fewer points on the teachers incremental scale which means that they go up the scale faster. In Southshire, schools have to appoint high up the scale in order to attract teachers to an area with very high housing costs. The problem is not unique to Southshire but applies to authorities around London that do not receive London weighting.

She also noted that the more general issue of lack of information feeding into the budget setting process was partly down to the delegation of budgeting to schools under local management of schools (LMS) set up by the 1988 Education Act. One problem with LMS, it seemed, was that LEAs had to 'stand back' with the result that they knew far less about schools than they used to as teachers and schools' employees were not necessarily on council payroll. The other apparent longer term problem was that special payments from central government had been targeted to poor performing schools, which were rare in Southshire.

There were no redundancies in Southshire schools, but problems arose from a non-replacement policy whereby 36 per cent schools had lost posts. Some schools, especially primary schools, had used money raised through voluntary activities for capital expenditure for salary/current expenditure. There had been no significant acts of defiance – no threats not to set budgets or to 'opt out of delegation'. There was still trust between the schools and the LEA, as the former accepted that the problem was not due to the LEA withholding funds.

Ironically, although the government had produced extra funding for schools and implicitly recognised that it had made mistakes, long run damage had been done to precisely those schemes that were good examples of modernised practices. For example, Southshire had an experimental social enhancement scheme, which had to be 'thrown out of the window'. This scheme channelled extra money to schools with problems such as 'low reading quotients'. The sophistication of the policy was that the idea was to monitor the effect of extra funding, but the experiment looked likely to stop due to short-run funding changes.

From a technical budgeting point of view, the general cause of the fiasco was the lack of knowledge about local cost drivers. Budgeting was very top-down. Schools submitted plans to the LEA every November, but 'always budget[ed] for a deficit', irrespective of real needs. Unsurprisingly, therefore, as the Chief educational officer noted, 'we have learnt not to rely on them'.

Budgetary problems in Southshire (II): Social service overspends

As in Eastmet, Southshire experienced budgetary overspends in its social services. The Head of Children's Services explained the perceived problem of a small number of looked-after children driving the budget. Problems were identified in terms of growth in this particular group, and the uncontrollable cost of placements:

> There's an element where you're reacting. This year the pressure has been fees. Teachers pay and conditions ... if an independent provider has to be replace windows – one school put its fees up by 90 per cent – the children's parents have a right of appeal if you un-lock placements. Once a statement says schools x.... You can't say its inappropriate on the basis of cost. Also, we haven't got enough in-home providers – foster carers. We want to start moving towards sustainability – enough resource to meet children needs.... At the moment we are spending ... 24 per cent of the budget on less than 1000 children.... Agency placements.... Because of the trend on fee indication.... If your resource level is constrained to RPI increases, you're.... Fees are going like that!! [draws a quick graph] It's the tail wagging the dog – you can't cut that provision if a court order they have to be therapeutic environment. But if you cut your (own) staffing, you're cutting the bulwark that stops them going into care in the first place. We're on the edge....

A long-term problem in Southshire was the difficulty in recruiting qualified social workers and foster carers to 'build capacity'. As the Head of Social services explained:

> Capacity building – Social workers at the front door, to do the assessment in the timescales (we get assessed on timescale not quality) ... we can't recruit social workers – its acute here.... we're whipping children out of families – but we haven't got capacity to check if someone else in the family could take them.... We lack the people ... so we're fostering .... And we haven't got the foster carers; sp we're using agency placements. So we need people, with the right skills mix.
>
> We also need diversionary capacity.... Not having to take the child... into care...a lot of people give up on children at 13 ... it's a big area of pressure ... we aim to give a ... support package. We divert them – avoid them coming into the system.... Prevention-moving them upstream. Getting less flowing through the gates. Like setting up kinship care, and .... family group conferences...

The Head was more critical of governmental attitudes than bitter about a lack of funding:

> I don't believe there isn't enough money in the system. But there are drivers pushing you in certain directions – cultural-and it takes a lot of professional discipline to break that down. ... you're never going to get wider knowledge or ownership of your budget. One child of 7 ... no parents ... a placement cost of £250K per year.... We're institutionalising him.... What are we getting.... What's the package ... the social worker went and asked and thought it would be less damaging to keep him where he is ... The culture is to respond to the individual need of the child ... but there are very precise legislation drivers The government and the politicians are so dishonest ... all this bollocks about choice...

The expenditure on old people seemed to be more predictable and easier to control. The council had a model that predicted how many old people in care homes would die. There are, however, also political pressures. As the Chief Finance Officer in the service area put it:

> There's a huge turnover paying for 2000 older people every year.... There are very tight eligibility criteria – that is our control mechanism ... the law says anyone who has social care needs can present themselves and we have to assess their needs. The criteria match money accurately to those needs. You basically

> ratchet the line up. You have to be 85 with a significant physical or mental health problem, that's our control mechanism. So there are huge number of people local teams are saying no to. You'd be horrified at people we leave in their own homes. Local managers are constantly saying no and people in management hold the line, then it goes to Members, and the Director turns round and says: pay for this person. Its very demoralising for the teams.

The link between the budget and non-financial information was quite sophisticated as he explained:

> We have a profile and we use information from the previous 2 years for the death rate to model the type of places ... we take a risk in assessing deaths in a month and saying that the Teams can make placements, up to a certain value. There's a review and tweaking of profiles each month to bring it back to budget.

Conclusions

The atmosphere surrounding the management of the budget in Southshire often seemed to reflect the quiet confidence of the local area with its neat suburbs and attractive countryside. Yet the fieldwork had picked up some problems, which could easily have been obscured behind the appearance of calm efficiency. In this respect, Southshire was almost a victim of its own success. A more crisis ridden polity may have had the effect of raising the public profile of the authority and enable it to demonstrate its importance in maintaining the affluent infrastructure of the county.

5

Comparisons and Conclusions

In this final chapter there is a comparison of the two cases as described in Chapters 3 and 4. The comparison is placed in the national context of local government budgeting as described in Chapter 2, which is updated to the end of the project in late 2003. It was particularly interesting to see how the national government responded to emerging problems in local government finance. It was also evident that although both the authorities were subject to the same regulatory regimes (as set out in Chapter 2), the geographical, economic, demographic and structural differences between them meant that they faced different financial circumstances and responded in different ways.

The national picture

On 10 December 2003, a £340 million increase in local government grants was announced in addition to the main settlement announced on November 19, 2003. The government had been rattled by the political backlash against the above inflation rises in council tax and was anxious to avoid similar rises before the next election. Emphasising his administration's generosity, Nick Raynsford, Minister for Local Government, pointed out to the House of Commons that:

> The provisional settlement I am announcing today will be the seventh successive one giving an above inflation increase in funding for local government. It will therefore build on the significant real terms growth we have been able to provide since taking office; grants to local government have increased by 29 per cent in real terms since 1997. This contrasts with a 7 per cent real terms cut in the last 4 years of the last government.

Although the overall context of expansion in local government funding must be born in mind when the changes in budgetary practices are evaluated, two caveats should also be noted. First, although the national government raised aggregate levels of funding to local government, the distribution of the increases varied with a general favouring of the metropolitan authorities in the north and midlands over the southern shire counties. Second, national government also raised its expectations for performance from local authorities so that although resources were increased, demands were also increased. As Raynsford put it in his speech to the House of Commons:

> We continue to consider carefully whether Government policies impose new spending burdens on local government, and make provision to fund them if they do.

Further, in the light of the sporadic protests against council tax rises, Raynsford issued this warning to local authorities:

> We are clear that the current trend in council tax rises is not sustainable. People expect their local councils to set reasonable council tax levels. They and we are looking to authorities to deliver high quality services in a cost-effective way. Against the background of further substantial increases in government grant, and the extension of freedoms and flexibilities to local authorities, large council tax increases are simply not acceptable.

Why were council tax rises so high?

A special study by the Audit Commission (2003) argued that there were two main reasons for the council tax increases. First, council spending went up more than expected. Secondly, as already pointed out, the low proportion of funding raised by local taxes *gears up* increases in expenditure so that typically a 1 per cent increase in spending increases council tax by 4 per cent. Whilst the Commission found no link between political control and rises in taxes, they found that lower than average grants were associated with higher than average tax rises. The Audit Commission (2003) also noted the external pressures on councils that pushed up spending as follows:

- public expects that services will improve;
- pressure from central government to spend more to meet government priorities;
- the role of inspectorates and other regulators in requiring councils to meet more demanding standards.

Fieldwork in the case studies corroborated the Commission's general findings, even though, as can be seen in Figure 5.1, the cost pressures were not identical.

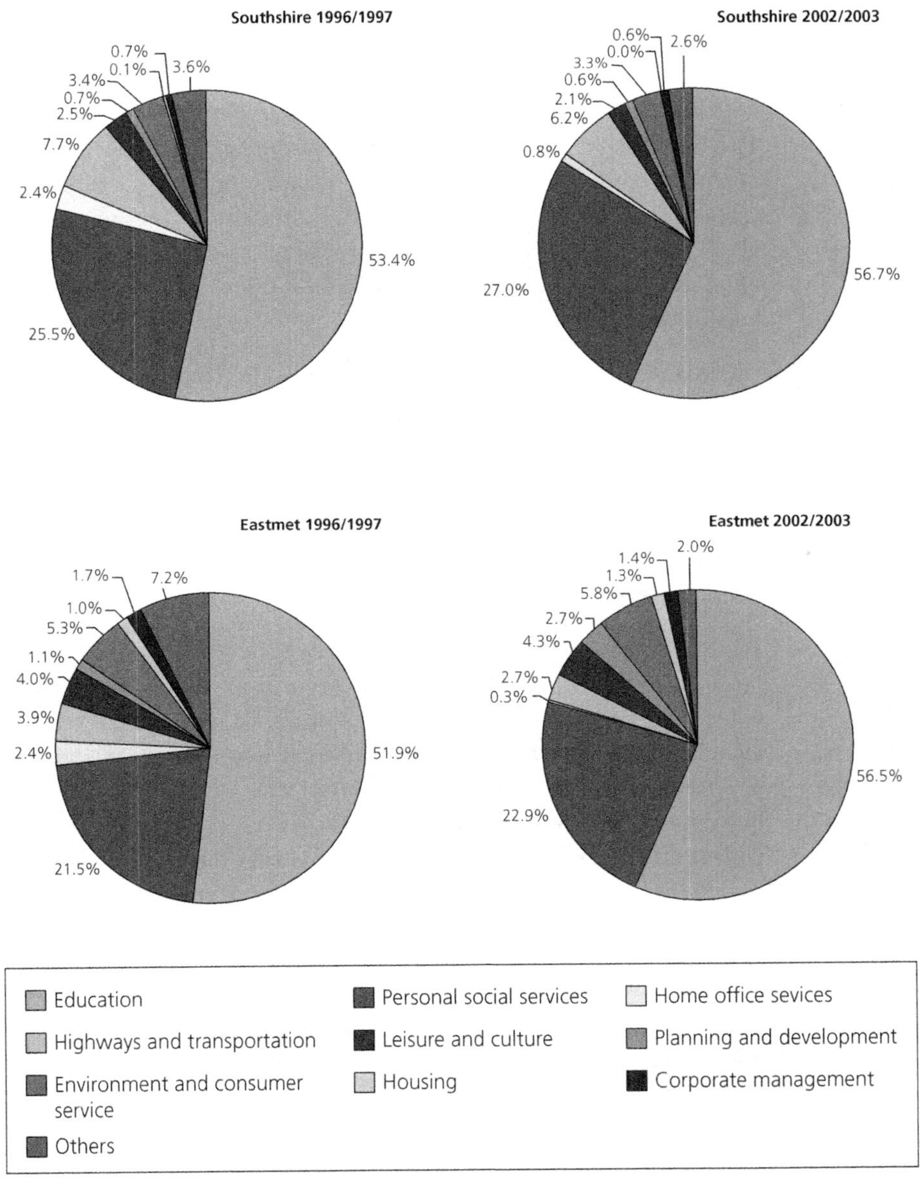

Figure 5.1 Percentage change in service expenditure.
Source: CIPFA Statistical Information Services

Education funding

Potentially more politically damaging (especially for the ministers of education), the so-called 'schools funding fiasco' led to some quite unusually candid admissions from the Department for Education and Skills (DFES) which acknowledged that it had made significant errors in changing schools funding arrangements. A report on the schools funding crisis produced by the House of Commons select committee stated that:

> The Secretary of State and his officials told us that they were unable to model the effects of this year's funding changes to the schools level, and we acknowledge the difficulties. It was, however, a serious weakness in the Department's strategy to implement the funding changes without knowing how schools would be affected. (2003, p. 7).

One significant aspect of this admission is that local authorities had successfully resisted the earlier attempts by the DFES to blame Local Education Authorities for the financial problems of schools. A second aspect concerns *an area where the expertise of management accounting should be able to make a contribution*: the development of a disaggregated cost model for schools. The select committee put it as follows:

> The DFES needs to have information from schools as well as LEAs in order to gain the full picture, and it needs information other than simply teacher numbers. The DFES, Parliament and all other interested parties need hard evidence about what has happened across the country in order to make judgements about how to proceed. Without that hard evidence, the perception of a widespread funding crisis will persist whatever the real position is, and that is damaging for the whole schools system (2003, p. 7).

This problem was picked up in the field work where it was found that in spite of the administrative changes in terms of schools forums, the effective level of school participation in the funding cycle was very low. In both case authorities, education service accountants were forced to discount the input from schools in terms of their proposed budgets because schools invariably budgeted for a loss. Thus the problem was not that there was no formal mechanism for participation, but that schools' plans lacked credibility owing to a history of 'crying wolf'.

Local statistical trends and comparisons

Although the period 1997–2003 has (at least until recently) been portrayed as being a phase of severe restraint ruled over by an 'Iron Chancellor', local public expenditure increased by 38 per cent in Eastmet and by 68 per cent in Southshire in real terms. From the point of view of budgeting practice, this sort of growth should have given both authorities the chance to substantially change the mix of expenditures. As may be seen from Figure 5.1, there was some change in the relative proportions, with Eastmet increasing the proportion spent on education from 52 per cent to 57 per cent compared with Southshire where education spending rose from 53 per cent to 57 per cent. The similarity between these increases and relative proportions is interesting when checked against the perceived priorities in the two authorities. Eastmet had made an explicit pledge to increase its education spending. In contrast, Southshire without making the same public commitment ended with a strikingly similar relative effort. More probably, the most significant driver of the relative increase in education spending was that both authorities responded to the priority given to education by national government.

Homogeneity versus diversity

Three powerful forces that can lead to homogeneity between local authorities are *coercive, mimetic* and *normative* (DiMaggio and Powell, 1983). Coercion refers in particular to central government regulation and inspection. Services in Eastmet and Southshire were regulated on the basis of a national policy of reducing rather than encouraging geographical variations in standards. Financial management tools such as general and ring fenced grants were intended to homogenise, not encourage diversity. Mimetic behaviour refers to the tendency of organisations to imitate each other. Modernisation policies, particularly benchmarking (Bowerman and Ball, 2001), have encouraged authorities to compare performance and practices on an increasingly rigorous basis. It was evident from the fieldwork that it would have been extremely unlikely for Eastmet and Southshire to benchmark each other, although they each had identified comparator authorities (i.e. with similar geographic, economic and demographic profiles to themselves).

Normative forces refer to the influence of professional norms that are developed and promulgated by accounting bodies. In the fieldwork, the most influential body was the Chartered Institute of Public Finance and Accountancy (CIPFA), which was the predominant qualification for the finance professionals that were interviewed.

More indirect professional influence came from the auditors who employed personnel with a variety of professional qualifications. Indeed, local government has an immense and generally unheralded reservoir of financial and managerial expertise that is drawn upon by central government and other public bodies such as the Audit Commission.

The diversity in budgeting practices in the cases came from the stark contrast in the contingency factors that distinguished Eastmet and Southshire. The most important driver of diversity was the immense difference in the economic circumstances between Eastmet and Southshire. Whilst Eastmet faced challenges of de-industrialisation, unemployment and general economic decline, Southshire's problems were outcomes of affluence with issues of congestion and labour shortages. Eastmet also had a stronger sense of locality with a vibrant local media and lively political culture. From a moderniser's perspective whilst Eastmet's problem was 'too much politics', Southshire's faced the opposite problem of struggling to find an identity. This struggle was captured by a comment made by the deputy head of Southshire council:

> The whole of the Local Government Act 2000 gives local authorities a last ditch opportunity, especially the County Councils and we need to rise to the challenge of being Community Leaders and really get to the heart of local government. It's not about the whole series of services.... It's not just a collection of service providers. Anybody could run a care service or a library. You could outsource the whole lot. We're different because of the fundamental democratic structure, which is worth fighting for. The alternative is a centralist regime (regionalist ... whatever). And the loss of a whole series of things.

Diversity is not simply a passive response to differing circumstances; leadership and strategy can make a difference even in the UK system of local government. For example in Eastmet, the Head of Performance and Scrutiny emphasised the key influence of the Chief executive:

> What's helped drive this (modernization) is the Chief Executive – he wanted a performance culture and accountability. If you're going to be a high performing authority, you need to know where you are ... the inspection should be a reality check.

Commonalities in developing budgeting practices

Having updated the regulatory and policy framework that was introduced in Chapter 2, this chapter will now look at the developments in the case authorities. Although some of the developments were driven by modernisation policies, other changes in practice could be attributed to local initiatives.

New political and management structures

The old management structures were almost inevitably incrementalist with big departments that were in alliance with specialised committees. Both case study authorities had abolished departmental structures and had adopted small cabinets, with senior members holding portfolios that reflect a cross-cutting perspective. In Southshire, for example, there was now a single organisational structure and budget for children's services, replacing the old education and social service departments.

An increased use of policy-led budgeting

Both authorities had developed long- and medium-term plans that were intended to indicate the councils' priorities and guide long-term financial strategies. In Eastmet, finance officers aided the different political groupings to formulate their own budgets. Budget options were presented to members at beginning of the budgetary cycle in order to create capacity rather than rely on savings at the back end of the cycle. The overall aim in both authorities was to embed corporate priorities into the budgetary process.

An increased use of non-financial performance indicators in conjunction with financial measures

Both authorities had developed new reporting systems that not only picked up the traditional budgetary variances but also monitored non-financial performance. Both authorities had also developed three-year financial strategies with special mechanisms to allow investment in services and promote changes in service provision. Not only had budgetary submissions to be couched in terms of corporate priorities but they also had to be related to measurable outcomes. These developments had been encouraged by the Comprehensive Performance Assessment (CPA) methodology, which extended performance measurement from individual service areas to corporate activities such as planning and performance measurement. Both authorities had also begun to invest heavily in more sophisticated information technologies such as Enterprise Resource Planning (ERP) that enabled greater integration of diverse data bases.

Services (and their budgets) were subject to periodic fundamental reviews

Incrementalism is associated with a tendency to just roll over existing budgets without asking whether the underlying activities that are being financed are still necessary or the most effective way of providing local government services. Best Value institutionalised a programme of periodic reviews. Southshire had a member-led approach to fundamental review that had actually anticipated the Best Value philosophy. In Eastmet, finance managers were introducing a system of Base Budget Review, which followed the principle of reviewing service budgets to see whether it was possible to 'take lines out'.

What is the extent to which is it possible or useful to reform incrementalist budgeting practices?

The preceding section outlined four important commonalities in evolving budgeting practices in Eastmet and Southshire. These developments in budgeting practice over the six-year period lead us to conclude that there were indeed significant attempts over the period to *reform* incrementalist budgeting practices. In general, officials in both authorities displayed an attitude of not only wanting to embrace change but actually influence it by putting up their own proposals and through networking with other local authorities in the area. Accordingly it seemed to us that managers and councillors alike were judging shifts in budgetary practice to be *useful as well as possible*. Financial and service managers at Eastmet and Southshire could justifiably argue that much of the modernising legislation was simply an embodiment of good practice in the sector. From this perspective some of the initiatives in cross-cutting services and reviewing programmes were in advance of national government reforms. Furthermore, national government quite often did not 'practice what it preached'.

As explained in the case chapters, each authority faced difficulties in the areas of education and personal social services. By focusing on these particularly pressured areas, the research homed in factors explaining why change in incrementalist budgetary practice was judged to be so critical.

Both authorities experienced difficulties in controlling spending in the area of children's social services but were developing coping strategies and evolving budgeting practice. For example, both saw the way forward as visibly building capacity, which involved saving future cost rises through spending now. These strategies were enabled both by a wider development of strategic capacity through the cabinet model and through both local and central governments embracing the philosophy of medium-term financial planning.

Paradoxically, it was in education spending where the medium-term outlook was obscured by short-falls in schools funding-caused by national government's technical weaknesses in budgeting. It must be acknowledged, of course, that from a budgeting perspective, local management of schools has meant that *both* local and central governments have lost knowledge on the schools cost drivers. The research project saw some of the knock-on effects of the schools cash crisis in terms of the increased funding described above. Indeed, until better schools budgeting is effected through increasingly participative mechanisms, including schools forums, it is likely there will be repeats of the 2003 funding debacle.

A concurrent significant pressure working against attempts to develop alternatives to incrementalist budgeting is the situation whereby on average local authorities only raise about 25 per cent of their income through local taxes. This leads to a gearing effect whereby a 5 per cent increase in total expenditure implies a much higher percentage increase in council tax in order to finance it. Southshire suffered in particular from a deliberate national policy of re-allocating local government funding away from the south of England to the Midlands and the North.

In Eastmet, officials and members were also learning how to manage contractually based education services in a situation where contractual governance had effectively been mandatorily imposed on them. In Southshire, moves towards contractualisation were more voluntary and incremental. In both authorities, finance professionals had had to acquire new skills of contract negotiation and monitoring, often on a learning-by-doing basis.

Conclusion and recommendations

In summary, it seemed that the authorities singled out for this study had the political will, as well as managerial and technical competence, to reform incrementalist budgeting practices. From a perspective concerned with better budget practice in local government, and based on the key observations from out study, we make the following recommendations:

- There is a need for more participation in local budgeting especially a more credible system for schools to get involved in the budget setting process.
- If the system is to remain centralised or even become more centralised then policy makers need to have a better knowledge of educational cost drivers.
- There needs to be a more even handed approach to outsourcing. At present, modernisation seems to be associated with outsourcing rather than on a rational appraisal of 'make or buy' which might suggest bringing some services back in-house.
- In connection with the above point, the authorities were developing necessary skills in contract negotiation and monitoring on a rather *ad hoc* basis. Since these areas seemed to be seen as the responsibility of finance staff, professional accounting bodies should perhaps place more explicit emphasis on training their members in these skills.
- The government should practice more of what it preaches. Policy at central government level is not joined up with damaging rivalry between ministries such as the Office of the Deputy Prime Minister and the DFES.
- Local authorities had developed a more strategic approach to their financial management but national government should acknowledge that strategising will almost inevitably be hindered by short-term variations in central government support.

As the Blair era and the all talk of a 'Third Way' have become part of political history, it will be interesting to see the future role of local government in the United Kingdom. It might be hoped that when council taxes rise quickly, central government will be less quick to 'scapegoat' local government for problems that are the responsibility of central rather than local government. For its part, local government should try to improve its public image in many areas it is doing a very good job. It has 're-invented' itself but the knowledge and nature of the improvements are not as widely appreciated as they should be. Our research left us with the hope that the many benefits that accrue from the decentralisation of political power to elected and reformed local bodies will eventually get their due recognition.

References

Audit Commission (1999) *Planning to Succeed: Service and Financial Planning in Local Government*, Audit Commission, London.

Audit Commission (2002) *The Comprehensive Performance Assessment Framework for Single Tier and County Councils*, Audit Commission, London.

Audit Commission (2003) *Council Tax Increases 2003/04: Why were They so High?*, Audit Commission Local Government Briefing, London.

Audit Commission (2004) *Education Funding: The Impact and Effectiveness of Measures to Stabilise School Funding*, Audit Commission, London.

Ball, A., Broadbent, B. and Jarvis, T. (2006) Waste Management, the Challenges of the PFI and Sustainability Reporting. *Business Strategy and the Environment*, 15(4), 258–274.

Benington, J., Bovaird, T., Geddes, M., Hartley, J., Lewis, M., Sanderson, I. and Sapwell, P. (1999) Evaluating Best Value: Approaches to the Monitoring and Evaluation of the National Best Value Pilot Programme, *Warwick/DETR Best Value Series Paper No. 3.* (University of Warwick).

Bowerman, M. and Ball, A. (2001) *The State of Benchmarking in the UK Local Government Sector*, Chartered Institute of Management Accountants, London.

Broadbent, J. and Laughlin, R. (2005) The role of PFI in the UK Government's modernisation agenda. *Financial Accountability and Management*, 21(1), 75–97.

Bromwich, M. and Lapsley, I. (1997) Decentralisation and management accounting: Recycling old ideas?. *Financial Accountability and Management*, 13(2), 181–201.

Chandler, J.A. (2001) *Local Government Today (3e)*, Manchester University Press, Manchester.

Department of Environment, Transport and Regions (DETR) (1998) *Modern Local Government: In Touch with the People,* White Paper, July, London.

Department of Environment, Transport and Regions (1999) *Best Value Performance Plans: Practice and Procedures,* White Paper, December, London.

Department for Transport, Local Government and the Regions (2000) Modernising Local Government Finance: A Green Paper, September, London.

Department of Local Government, Transport and Regions (DLTR) (2001) *Strong Local Leadership – Quality Public Services*, London.

DiMaggio, P. and Powell, W. (1983) The iron cage re-visited: Institutional isomorphism and collective rationality in organizational fields. *American Sociological Review*, 48, 147–160.

Ezzamel, M., Robson, K., Stapleton, P. and McLean, C. (2007) Discourse and institutional change: 'Giving accounts' and accountability. *Management Accounting Research*, 18, 150–171.

Filkin, G., Allen, E. and Williams, J. (2001) *Strategic Partnering for Local Service Delivery*, NLGN publications, London.

Giddens, A. (1998) *The Third Way*, Polity Press, Cambridge.

Guthrie, J., Humphrey, C., Jones, L.R. and Olson, O. (Eds.) (2005) *International Public Management Reform: Progress, Contradictions and Challenges*. Information Age Publishing, Greenwich, Connecticut.

Hale, R. and Capaldi, A. (2003) *Councillors' Guide to Local Government Finance*, CIPFA, London.

Hetherington, P. (2004) Council tax rebels march on Whitehall. *The Guardian*, January 17, 6.

Hood, C. (1995) The 'new public management' in the 1980's: Variations on a theme. *Accounting, Organizations and Society*, 20(2/3), 93–109.

House of Commons Education and Skills Committee (2003) *Public Expenditure: Schools' Funding: First Report of Session 2003–04* (HC112; 18 December 2003, The Stationary Office Limited, London).

Hurst, G. (2004) Rich to pay for radical reform of council tax. *The Times*, January 12, 1.

Jones, C.S. (2002) The attitudes of British National Health Service Managers and Clinicians Towards the Introduction of Benchmarking, *Financial Accountability Management*, 18(2), 163–188.

Leach, S. and Charteris, S. (2000) Managing the budgetary process in a hung council. *Public Administration*, 78(4), 793–814.

Local Government Association (LGA) (2004) *Building on Success: A Second Generation of Local Public Service Agreements*, LGA, London.

Martin, S. (1998) Achieving Best Value through Public Engagement, *Warwick/DETR Best Value Series, Paper No. 8.*

Mayston, D. (1998) Devolved budgeting, formula funding and equity. *Management Accounting Research*, 8, 37–54.

Olson, O., Guthrie, J. and Humphrey, C. (Eds.) (1998) *Global Warning! Debating International Developments in New Public Management Financial Management*, Cappelen Akademisk Forlag, Oslo.

Pollock, A. (2004) *NHS plc*, Verso, London.

Scapens, R. (1990) Researching management accounting practice: The role of case study research. *British Accounting Review*, 22, 259–281.

Seal, W. (1999) Accounting and Compulsory Competitive Tendering: An Institutionalist Interpretation of the New Public Management in UK Local Government. *Financial Accountability and Management*, 15(3&4), 309–327.

Seal, W. (2003) Modernity, modernization and the deinstitutionalisation of incremental budgeting in local government. *Financial Accountability and Management Journal*, 19(2), 93–116.

Shaoul, J. (2005) A critical financial analysis of the Private Finance Initiative: Selecting a financing method or allocating economic wealth?. *Critical Perspectives on Accounting*, 16(4), 441–471.

Stewart, J. (2000) *The Nature of British Local Government*, Macmillan, Basingstoke, Hampshire, UK.

Stoker, G. (1996) The Struggle to Reform Local Government: 1970–95. *Public Money and Management*, 16(1), 17–22.

Walsh, K. (1995) *Public Services and Market Mechanisms: Competition, Contracting and the New Public Management*, Macmillan, London.

Wildavsky, A. (1975) *Budgeting: A Comparative Theory of Budgetary process*, Little Brown, Boston.

Notes

1 We are grateful to an anonymous referee for this observation.
2 In order to help to preserve the anonymity of the council some of the numbers have been altered. Although we draw on the council's original documents we cannot attach full version in the appendices.
3 Source: Eastmet Corporate Assessment.
4 Quoted from an internal Eastmet document.
5 The Lamming report was set up to report on protection of vulnerable children after the murder of Victoria Climbie.
6 The post of Head of Education Finance was vacated and re-filled during the currency of the research. We therefore refer of Head of Education Finance (I) and Head of Education Finance (II) in this Chapter.

Index

Printed in Dunstable, United Kingdom

91900959R00058